ŚABDA PRAMĀṆA—AN EPISTEMOLOGICAL ANALYSIS

SRI GARIB DASS ORIENTAL SERIES NO 58

SABDA PRAMĀNA

AN EPISTEMOLOGICAL ANALYSIS

R. I. INAGALALLI

SRI SATGURU PUBLICATIONS
DELHI—INDIA

Published by :
SRI SATGURU PUBLICATIONS

A division of :
INDIAN BOOKS CENTRE
Indological and Oriental Publishers
40/5, Shakti Nagar,
DELHI - 110007
(INDIA)

First Edition :—DELHI—1988

I.S.B.N.—81-7030—120-3

Printed in India :
Composed by AMAR PRINTERS
1332/90, Tri Nagar, Delhi-35.
Printed by Kiran Mudran Kendra
A-38/2, Mayapuri, Phase I
New Delhi

CONTENTS

ACKNOWLEDGEMENT *vii*

ABBREVIATIONS AND CONVENTIONS *ix-xi*

CHAPTERS

INTRODUCTION 1-8

1. WHAT IS KNOWLEDGE ? 9-15
2. PRAMĀ AS KNOWLEDGE (I) 16-32
3. PRAMĀ AS KNOWLEDGE (II) 33-58
4. WHAT IS PRAMĀṆA ? 59-65
5. INDEPENDENCE OF A PRAMĀṆA 66-73
6. ŚABDA-PRAMĀṆA 74-80 74-80
7. VAIDIKA ŚABDA 81-93
8. INDEPENDENCE OF ŚABDA PRAMĀṆA 94-100
9. VAIDIKA ŚABDA, REVELATION, AND REASON 101-106
10. VAIDIKA ŚABDA AND CRITERIA OF TRUTH (I) 107-118
11. VAIDIKA ŚABDA AND CRITERIA OF TRUTH (II) 119-125
12. CONCLUSION 126-141

ADDENDUM : SCRIPTURAL TESTIMONY 142-148

BIBLIOGRAPHY 149-156

SANSKRIT INDEX 157-158

ENGLISH INDEX 159-160

ACKNOWLEDGEMENT

This thesis is an attempt at interpreting the traditional concept of Śabda pramāṇa in contemporary epistemological terms. There are not many works of this type and I have tried to contribute my mite to the clarification of this concept which has played such a vital role in the development of Indian thought. I have completed this work under the guidance of Dr. L.C. Mullatti, Chairman of the Department of Philosophy, Karnatak University, Dharwad. I am immensely grateful to him for all the help and encouragement he has given me all through the thesis project. I owe to him even the thought of doing Ph. D. Right from that early stage he has put up with my foibles and deficiencies and heroically conducted me to my goal. He has helped me inside and outside the Department night and day, despite severe inconveniences to himself, and some times even at the cost of his own important academic work. Most of the important ideas that appear in this thesis bear his stamp and it is not an exaggeration to say that the work would not have been completed but for his unusually strong interest and commitment. It is needless to add that I alone am responsible for the deficiencies that might have remained in the thesis.

I am also grateful to the Karnatak University authorities for having offered me a U.G.C. Teacher Fellowship for four years. I should be failing in my duty if I do not acknowledge my appreciation to the other members of the Department of Philosophy, Karnatak University, and the staff of the Karnatak University Library for the help that I have received from them.

Finally, I record my gratitude to the authorities of the Veerashaiva Vidyavardhaka Sangh, Bellary, my employers (during 1972-85) for encouraging me in taking up this research work.

KARNATAK UNIVERSITY R.I. INGALALLI

DHARWAD (INDIA)

OCT. 1987.

ABBREVIATIONS AND CONVENTIONS

A. Abbreviations

(Titles of Books)

(a) Athalye=Athalye and Bodas 1974. References indicate page numbers.

(b) BP=*Bhāṣā-pariccheda* by Viśvanātha Nyāya Pañcānana. Included in Bhatta 1972a; 1972b. See Madhavananda 1977. References indicate sections.

(c) MN=*Mānameyodaya* by Nārāyaṇa. Included in Raja and Sastri 1975. References are to page numbers.

(d) MS=*Mīmāṃsa-sūtra of Jaimini*. Included in Sandal 1932. References are to individual verses.

(e) NBh=*Nyāya-bhāṣya* by Vātsyāyna. References are to sections. See (h) below.

(f) NK=*Nyāya-kośa*. See Jhalkikar 1978. References are by word entries.

(g) NM=*Nyāya-mañjarī* by Jayanta Bhaṭṭa. Included in Sukla 1971. See J.V. Bhattacharya 1978. References indicate page numbers.

(h) NS=Nyāya-sūtra by Gautama (with Nyāya-bhāṣya o Vātsyāyana). Included in Jha and Sastri 1925. See Jha 1939. References are to sections.

(i) SBBS=Śaṅkara's Bhāṣya on Brahma-sūtra. Included in Acharya 1948. See Gambhirananda 1972. References are to sections.

(j) SBBU=Śaṅkara's bhāṣya on Bṛhadāraṇyaka-upaniṣad. Included in Bhāgavata 1840. See Madhavananda 1975. References are to sections.

(k) SBKU=Śaṅkara's bhāṣya on Katha-upaniṣad. Included Bhāgavata 1840. See Gambhirananda 1977. References are to sections.

(l) SBMU=Śaṅkara's bhāṣya on Māṇḍukya-upaniṣad (with Kārika by Gauḍapāda). Included in Bhāgavata 1840. See Nikhilananda 1974. References are to sections.

(m) SM=*Siddhānta-muktāvalī* by Viśvanātha Nyāya pañcānana. Included in Bhatta 1972a, 1972b. See Madhavananda 1977. References are to sections.

(n) SP=*Sapta-padārthī* by Śivāditya. Included in Gurumurti 1932. References are to individual verses.

(o) TD=*Tarka-dīpikā* by Annaṃbhaṭṭa. See (p) below.

(p) TS=*Tarka-saṃgraha* (with *Tarka-dīpikā*) by Annaṃbhaṭṭa Included in Athalye and Bodas 1974. See Bhattacharya 1975. References indicate sections.

(q) VP=*Vedānta-paribhāṣā* by Dharmarāja Adhvarīndra. Included in Madhavananda 1972. Refercnces indicate page numbers.

B. Conventions

(a) *Translation*

When words are underlined and enclosed in brackets, it means that they are not part of the literal translation, but are needed to make the literal translation intelligible.

(b) *Quotes*

Single quotes are used to form names of single words and phrases. Double quotes are used (i) to isolate the English translation from the Sanskrit text, (ii) to show that the expression with quotes needs to be added to make the translation of a Sanskrit passage complete and (iii) to indicate that a quoted expression is used in an unusual way.

(c) *References*

References are to author's (or editor's or translator's) name, year of publication and page number(s), unless otherwise indicate under *Abbreviations* (Part A above). In the case of more than one publication by the same author in a given year, the year of publication is followed by the letters 'a' 'b' etc.

(d) *Cross References*

Section numpers consist of the capital letter 'S', followed by the number of the relevant chapter followed by the serial number of the section in the relevant chapter. For example, 'S 3.15' means section 15 of Chapter 3.

Cross references to notes consist of the letters *fn* followed by the relevant chapter number, followed by the serial number of the note in the relevant chapter. For example, 'fn 4.3' means note 3 of chapter 4.

INTRODUCTION

S 0.1 In the tradition of Indian thought, scriptural authority has always occupied an important position. Sometimes, the importance attached to it is so great that all other forms of knowledge are subordinated to it. By and large, however, it is given a position which is in harmony with the other forms of knowledge *i.e.*, those based on our experience or our reason. But it remains a baffling problem how scriptural authority as a source of knowledge can retain its independence and yet remain in harmony with other sources of knowledge. It is rather intriguing that this baffling problem has hardly invited a probing inquiry either from modern Indian thinkers or from traditional ones. Both these classes of thinkers behave as if there is no real problem. Śaṅkara, for example, says that even if hundred scriptures say that fire is cold, we must not accept such a statement.[1] In other words, Śaṅkara seems to imply that any thing that goes flagrantly against our generally accepted cognitive faculties is to be rejected even if it comes with the highest scriptural credentials. And the same position seems to be repeated even by respectable modern Indian thinkers like Hiriyanna (1973 : 179) and Devaraja (1972 : 53, 56). It is this situation that has prompted me to take up this problem for investigation in this dissertation. It is my aim to make precise the questions especially concerning scriptural authority and examine the answers that have been traditionally given to them and also the views of modern thinkers on these traditional answers. In pursuing this aim, I have mostly limited myself to the treatment of the subject dealt with in the two orthodox schools, namely, Nyāya and Advaita-vedānta. Occasional references to other schools are also made but only incidentally. Even with respect to these two schools, I cannot claim exhaustiveness, I have taken only four as representative of the works of these two schools as the basis of my inquiry. These are *Nyāya-mañjarī* (NM) by Jayanta Bhaṭṭa (965 A.D); *Tarka-saṅgraha* (TS) (with *Dīpika*—TD) by Annaṃbhaṭṭa (17th century A.D.); *Bhāṣā-pariccheda* (BP) (with *Siddhānta-muktāvalī*—SM) by Viśvanātha (17th century A.D.) and *Vedānta-paribhāṣā* (VP) by Dharmarāja Advarīndra (17th century).

S 0.2 Since scriptural authority is generally discussed under the rubric of testimony and since testimony is traditionally regarded as a promāṇa the question, what is pramāṇa ?, assumes importance for me. But an attempt to answer this question immediately leads to the question, what is pramā ?,[2] because pramāṇa is defined as the instrumental cause of pramā.[3] But a full appreciation of this latter question and the traditional answer to it is not possible unless a yardstick is developed to assess the situation and so I begin in the first chapter with a discussion of the nature of knowledge as it is understood today.

S 0.3 I consider what is called the modern classical definition of knowledge, namely, knowledge is justified true belief. Gettier's objections to this definition are examined and certain possible remedies are brought in. I conclude by emphasising that it is necessary to recognise that the statements in terms of which a belief is justified must be known to be true (not just true) in order that the belief in question should count as knowledge.

S 0.4 Having developed a yardstick in the form of the contemporary analysis of knowledge, I next raised the question whether pramā is the same as knowledge. I answer this question by asking in turn whether pramā satisfies the three basic conditions of knowledge *viz.*, the truth condition, the belief condition and the justification condition. As for the truth condition, it is pointed out that it is built into the very definition of pramā, namely, that it is yathārthānubhava (S 2.3). So the satisfaction of this condition of pramā is automatic, but the difficulty arises with regard to the belief condition. Since pramā is defined as true cognition, it would appear on the face of it that pramā is identical with truth but not with knowledge. While there is indeed no explicit evidence, as far as I know, for claiming that pramā satisfies the belief condition, there is ample implicit and indirect evidence. For instance, even the etymology of 'pramā' suggests that pramā involves belief also. The sources of pramā traditionally listed, namely, perception (pratyakṣa), inference (anumāna) etc. imply that the belief condition is fulfilled in pramā. They are human mechanisms of pramā. Pramā is at very least true cognition. If nothing else but pramā is what is processed in these mechanisms then belief in what is processed is surely entailed.

S 0.5 The question of the justification condition presents even greater difficulty, partly because of the total unawareness of this problem on the part of the traditional thinkers and partly because of the very sophisticated character of the problem. Here, too, therefore, resourse to indirect and contextual evidence is absolutely essential to resolve the question whether pramā satisfies the justification condition. I have tried to answer this question by raising it with reference to each of the several types of pramā. My finding is that the justification condition is indeed satisfied in the case of each type. This means that pramā on the whole satisfies that condition. Since pramā is found to satisfy the three basic conditions of knowledge, I conclude that pramā is in substance not different from knowledge.

S 0.6 This analysis of the logical character of pramā enables to investigate one of the basic questions of my dissertation, namely, what is pramāṇa ? The traditional definition of pramāṇa is : pramāṇa is the instrumental cause of pramā (fn 0.3). However, I have not dwelt upon the question, how best to understand the expression 'instrumental cause' in the epistemic contexts. Traditionally the term cause (kāraṇa) has been used very ambiguously and it is very difficult to keep out its psychological sense. In any case, it is my feeling that even if the use of that expression is discounted, not much is lost. Relying on the commonsense notion of a source of knowledge, I have examined the intriguing question whether pramāṇa is a source of knowledge only or of false beliefs as well. The reasons for and against the claim that pramāṇa is a source of knowledge only are considered. The upshot of this consideration is that the traditional thinkers indeed believed that pramāṇa is a source of knowledge only. This, of course, goes very much against the contemporary conception of a source of knowledge, but textual loyalty demands that we must recognise the views of traditional thinkers for what they are, whether they are right or wrong or whether we like them or not. The next question that is considered is what makes a pramāṇa independent or irreducible. Three traditional criteria in particular are considered. These are introspection (anuvyavasāya), novelty (anadhigatatva), and uniqueness of the objects(s) of knowledge. Introspection will not do as a criterion since a mere introspective (psychological) feeling can be no ground for the independent character of a pramāṇa. That such a character is logical and objective needs to be supported on logical and objective grounds. Novelty has to be dismissed since knowledge coming from a certain source may be novel and yet reducible, for example, in mundane testimony. It is the uniqueness of object(s) of knowledge which offers a plausible criterion. I formulate the criterion thus : A pramāṇa is independent if and only if there is at least one object which can be known by it alone and by no other pramāṇa. It is also pointed out that novelty is a consequence of uniqueness, though not conversely.

S 0.7 All this is really by way of preparing the ground for the main study, namely, an investigation into the logical character of śabda-pramāṇa. This study is now directly begun in Chapter VI. A commonly accepted definition of śabda is the one given by the Naiyāyikas. This definiton says that testimony (śabda) is the statement of a trustworthy person (āptavacana). The Naiyāyikas and Advaitins attach different significance to the expression 'āptavacana,' but this difference is in fact apparent and not real. How it is not real is clarified. It is shown that even vedic statements which according to Advaitins are authorless really come under āptavacana. It is also shown that in the case of the Naiyāyikas' view, the expression, 'āptavacana' is not limited to the utterances of human beings but is applicable equally well to Vedic statements even through these latter, according to the Naiyāyikas, are of divine authorship. In other words, I have tried to establish that the conception of testimony as 'āptavacana' is substantially the same in the case of both Naiyāyikas and Advaitins (and Bhāṭṭas).

S 0.8 After clarifying the nature of an āpta, I consider the question of how to identify him. What are, in other words, the tests or criteria of an āpta ? Vātsyāyana's answer to this question is that an āpta is one who possesses the relevant knowledge and the needed integrity, and who has the ability to communicate properly. In other words, Vātsyāyana lays down a three-fold criterion for an āpta : Adequate and relevant knowledge, integrity and the ability to communicate together constitute necessary and sufficient conditions of an āpta. This three-fold requirement is a good enough test of an āpta. But, of course, the decision whether a given person is a man of integrity or a man of knowledge has to be made inductively, and even the decision whether a man is capable of adequate communication is empirical though routine. A reference is made in this regard to Price's principle of testimony which brings out the inductive character of such decisions. A reference is also made to Montague's discussion of prestige, number and age as possible criteria and to his rejection of number and age in favour of prestige. It has been pointed out that his criterion of prestige really amounts to Vātsyāyana's criteria of knowledge and integrity.

S 0.9 The central topic of discussion concerning śabda pramāṇa is scriptural testimony (Vaidika śabda), and this topic is taken up in Chapter VII. The principal question that is considered there is whether or not the Veda is authored. The opposite views of the Naiyāyikas and the Mīmāṃsakas are stated and assessed. Further it is shown that the claim made by secondary authors like S. Murthy (S 7.28) and Athalye (S 7.28) that the Advaita position is a compromise between the pauruṣeyatā-vāda of the Naiyāyikas and the apauruṣeyatā-vāda of the Mīmāṃsakas really rests on a confusion between the Veda as pramāṇa and the Veda as pramā, and that once this confusion is clarified the question of a compromise no longer makes sense. I then show in the next chapter that the criterion of independence, namely, uniqueness of object developed in Chapter V is satisfied by scriptural testimony as well, and that, therefore, it can claim independent status as a pramāṇa. The next question that is considered in Chapter IX is the relationship of scriptural testimony to revelation and reason. It is an unquestioned assumption that Vedic statements are revealed. It, therefore, becomes imperative to consider what precisely is revelation. Hick's definition of revelation is considered, and it is explained how revelation differs from intuition. It is also pointed out that there is in the writings on this issue, a confusion between revelation as a process and revelation as a product. In so far as we wish to relate revelation to scriptural testimony it can only be taken in the sense of a process.

S 0.10 There is considerable discussion in traditional literature regarding the relation of reason to revelation; and authors like Śaṅkara are sometimes held up as champions of reason. I have tried to show that this misleading. Inspite of apparent and occasional emphasis on reason, the underlying truth consistently remains that reason can operate only within the framework of revealed truth; that reason only supplements revelation but never supplants it. The question whether or not the Veda is authored has important ramifications, and one of these is the nature of the criterion of truth. For instance, it is sometimes claimed that apauruṣeyatā of the Veda implies svataḥ-prāmāṇya-vāda, or the theory that truth is intrinsic to a given statement (S 10.1). For it is held that any defect in a statement is due to its having been authored and that its being authorless is a guarantee of its self-certifying character. Hence, because of this vital connection of the pauruṣeyatā or otherwise of the Veda with the question of the criterion of truth, I enter in Chapters X and XI on a discussion of the traditional theories regarding the nature of criteria of truth. These theories are svataḥ-prāmāṇya-vāda of the Advaitins and the Bhāṭṭas and the parataḥ-prāmāṇya-vāda of the Naiyāyikas. The traditional distinction between utpatti, jñapti and prakāśa is analysed and it is pointed out that utpatti and prakāśa are epistemologically irrelevant being either psychological or scholastic in character. It is only jñapti that is of real significance in the epistemological context, even though it is hard to keep out the other two elements in an exposition of the traditional views of jñapti. Having clarified the implication of the question of jñapti the position of svataḥ-prāmāṇya-vāda is stated and the reasons for and against it are also stated and assessed. An analogous account of parataḥ-prāmāṇya-vāda is then given. The charge of circularity against parataḥ-prāmāṇya-vāda is shown to be untenable on independent grounds. The Naiyāyikas' own reply to that charge is shown to bring out limitations of parataḥ-prāmāṇya-vāda, namely that it only holds with respect to certain classes of statements but not with respect to certain others. What the criterion is in respect of the latter classes of statements according to Naiyāyikas is not clear but there is no doubt that the criterion of fruitful activity advocated by the Naiyāyikas is not exhaustive.

The relationship of these two doctrines of svataḥ-prāmāṇya-vāda and parataḥ-prāmāṇya-vāda is considered. It is pointed out that they are not theories of the nature of truth but of the criteria of truth. Regarding the nature of truth both the camps seem to accept the same definition and that definition seems to identify truth with correspondence (S 11.9). But this leads to consequences which are shown to be rather puzzling. The views of S. Murty,

Mohanty, Chatterjee, Hiriyanna and Deutsch are considered in this regard, and they are found to be unacceptable.

S 0.11 The earlier chapters aim at a reconstruction in contemporary conceptual terms of the traditional theory of śabda-pramāṇa, especially of Vaidika śabda pramāṇa (scriptural testimony). The concluding chapter aims at an assessment of that reconstruction. Since the most vehement attack on the meaningfulness of religious language (which scriptural testimony obviously is) comes from logical positivists, and since the backbone of their attack is their criterion of meaning, a rather detailed estimate of that criterion is first given. Certain deficiencies even in the revised formulation, given by Ayer, of the principle of verification and some possible remedies to rectify them are considered. This is followed by an account of the revival in more sophisticated terms of the traditional defence of religion. In particular, the views of Broad, Mitchel, Crombie, Alston and Hick are assessed and rejected. The most significant and notable attempt to accommodate religion comes from later Wittgenstein. His theory of meaning as use is considered, and its relation to the concepts of language game and form of life noted. In the end, even this theory of meaning is found to be unacceptable. Just as the empiricist theories of meaning constitute the very backbone of the empiricist attack on religion, later Wittgenstein's theory of meaning as use is at the root of his attempt to accommodate religion. Since this later theory is found to be inadequate, it follows that Wittgenstein's attempt to accommodate religion is unsuccessful. The denial of cognitive status to religious discourse means the denial of such status to scriptual testimony as well. If scriptural testimony altogether lacks cognitive status then, it is concluded, all the tall traditional claims on its behalf must be without substance. It cannot be a genuine pramāṇa. However such a conclusion is untenable, for the authors like Quine and Swinburne have argued that scriptural sentences are cognitively meaningful. Quine for instance has shown that scriptural sentences are also bearers of truth values. Consequently the cognitive character of scriptural language enables us to justify our knowledge claims involving scriptural statements. Thus Śabda-pramāṇa even in its non-sensuous form can also be treated as pramāṇa.

Notes and References

1. na śāstraṃ padārthānanyathā kartuṃ pravarattamkiṃ tarhi yathābhūtānāmajñātānām jñāpane. . .nahi agniḥ śītā āditya na tapatīti vā dṛṣṭāntaśatenāpi pratipādayituṃ. Śakyaṃ pramāṇātareṇānyathādhigatatvādvas tunaḥ. "The scriptures seek not to alter things but to supply information about thingsunknown, as they are. . . . You cannot prove that fire is cold, or that the sun does not not give heat, even by citing a hunndred examples, for the facts would already be known to be otherwise through another means of knowledge." SBBU 2.1.20. Translated by Madhavananda 1975:209.

2. I deliberately abstain from using here the usual English equivalent 'knowledge' until, I consider the question of its adequacy. This is done when I investigate the relationship of pramā with the contemporary concept of knowledge (S 3.27).

3. pramā karaṇaṃ pramāṇam. VP 4; Cf. NM 12; TD 36; SM 135.

1

WHAT IS KNOWLEDGE ?

S 1.1 In both Nyāya and Advaita systems scriptural authority is subsumed under testimony (śabda) and testimony is regarded as one of the pramāṇas (sources of pramā[1]). In fact this is so in the other orthodox schools also except Vaiśeṣika. As a preliminary, therefore to understanding what is testimony, it is necessary, to understand the nature of a pramāṇa. A pramāṇa has been traditionally defined as the instrumental cause of pramā (fn 0.3). Thus the process of regression is carried even further; now I have to answer the question, what is pramā? to be able to understand testimony and scriptural authority via the notion of pramāṇa. What then is pramā ? The well known Indian answer to this question is : "Pramā is that cognition which corresponds to reality."[2]

But a full appreciation of this apparently simple answer requires the development of a viewpoint from which to assess it. And the viewpoint can only be provided by an analysis of the concept of knowledge as it is understood today. I, therefore, have to answer first the question, what is knowledge in general ? Such an analysis constitutes the most fundamental problem of contemporary epistemology, and I have to tackle it first before I further elaborate on pramā.

S 1.2 What then is knowledge ? In an attempt to answer the question what exactly is knowledge it will be helpful to note certain aspects of the usage of the word 'knowledge'. The word 'knowledge' is not always used in the same way. There are two main uses of the word 'to know'. These are : (i) 'knowing how' and

(ii) 'knowing that'. 'Knowing how' is used in contexts where a person's ability to perform certain type of activity is considered ; for instance, 'knowing how to type letters or to swim etc.' But 'knowing that' is used in a propositional sense, *i.e.*, 'knowing that p' where p is a proposition. I am concerned only with 'the propositional sense' *i.e.*, the sense of 'knowing that'. It is this sense alone that is involved in the traditional Indian discussion of testimony (śabda).

S 1.3 A standard modern definition of knowledge (where knowledge is understood in the propositional sense) is that 'it is justified true belief'. This is also called the modern classical definition. According to this definition of knowledge considered by contemporary epistemologists[3] where 'S' is any knowing subject and p any proposition, S knows that p, if and only if

(i) p is true.
(ii) S believes that p,
and (iii) S is justified in believing that p.

Thus the above definition involves three important conditions: (i) Truth condition, (ii) Belief condition, and (iii) Justification condition.

(i) *Truth condition* :

The truth condition means that it is necessarily the case that the proposition known is true. In other words, "I know that p" entails that p; in still other words, to say that S knows that p and yet to maintain that p is not true is self contradictory. The sentence "if S knows that p then that p" is analytic since its truth depends solely on the meaning of the word 'know'. The truth condition is thus built into the very meaning of the word 'know'. If there is some reason to say that the proposition p is false, this immediately calls in the question of the relevant knowledge claim. But this does not of course mean that what is true must necessarily be known. Truth is independent of knowledge, but not conversely. In other words the truth condition is a necessary but not a sufficient condition of knowledge.

(ii) *Belief condition* :

This condition means a certain attitude namely, attitude of

entertaining a proposition p. If S knows that p, S must entertain that p. Like the truth condition the belief condition also is a necessary but not a sufficient condition of knowledge. As in the case of the truth condition, in the case of the belief condition also to make a knowledge claim and yet to deny belief would be self contradictory. But the relation between truth and belief is not the same as that between truth and knowledge. As stated above what is known must be true though not conversely. But both belief and truth can be independent of each other, in other words what is believed may not be true and what is true may not be believed. However, in a knowledge situation what is believed must be true. As before the sentence 'if S knows that p then S believes that p' is analytic.

(iii) *Justification condition* :

The truth condition and the belief condition are straightforward enough; they usually do not cause any problem regarding their meaning in a knowledge situation. But the justification condition is rather complicated and it is not at all easy to formulate what precisely it involves. The nature of the type of justification involved in knowledge is best understood by considering certain important objections arising out of the justification condition of the classical analysis. These objections are most powerfully voiced by Gettier (1963 : 121-3). Gettier's objections are mainly in the form of two counter examples. These two counter examples, primafacie at least, go against the classical analysis of the concept of knowledge stated above. In other words, all the three conditions, namely, the truth condition, the belief condition, and the justification condition may be fulfilled in a given case and yet the case in question may not constitute knowledge. Gettier's first example which I call A, may be briefly summarised as follows : Smith who is in search of a job reliably learns from his potential employer that Jones, another job seeker, will get the job. Smith also happens to have counted ten coins in Jones' pocket. On the basis of this evidence he is justified in accepting the following two statements :

1. Jones is the man who gets the job.
2. Jones has ten coins in his pocket.

But (1) and (2) logically yield

3. The man who gets the job has ten coins in his pocket. Now (3) is not a case of knowledge even though on the classical analysis of knowledge, it can be said to be justified true belief. For it so happens that unknown to Smith himself, Smith gets the job, and also unknown to himself Smith has ten coins in his pocket. It is this evidence which makes (3) true and not the evidence represented by (1) and (2). But of this evidence, Smith is totally unaware and bases (3) solely on (1) and (2). Hence (3) cannot be said to be known by Smith. But Smith may be said to be justified in believing (3), since it logically follows from (1) and (2) which Smith is justified in believing p. Gettier's second example is along the same lines and need not be considered here.

S 1.4 There are two main types of reactions to such counter examples. One type is represented by Clark (1963 : 44-7), Chisholm (1977 : 103-4) and Hamlyn (1977 : 81). It consists in accepting that Gettier's example A is indeed a counter example to the classical analysis of the concept of knowledge; that in other words the classical analysis is incomplete and hence inadequate. The classical analysis, according to this type of reaction does not specify all the necessary conditions that are presupposed in a knowledge situation. Its proponents, therefore, go on to add a fourth condition to the conditions mentioned in the classical analysis, namely;

(iv) The statement(s) which S uses to justify p must be true.

The proponents of this line of reasoning think that by the addition of this fourth condition the classical analysis is secured against any counter example. In particular, Gettier's example A ceases to be a counter example on the addition of this fourth condition. This is so because in that example (3) is justified in terms of the conjunction of (1) and (2) which (conjunction) is false, since (1) is false. Thus A violates the fourth condition and cannot lay claim to have complete compliance of the requirements of a knowledge situation.

The second type of reaction to Gettier's counter examples is represented by thinkers like Armstrong (1973 : 152-3), Pollock (1974 : 47) and Thalberg (1969 : 794-803). It consists in denying that the sense of the term 'justification' involved in these counter examples is the one intended in the classical analysis. The thrust of this line of argument is summarily to dismiss Gettier's examples, as being not even relevant. But what according to these people is the intended sense of 'justification' involved in the classical analysis ? Before answering this question it is pertinent to note that in the ultimate analysis the upshot of both these types of reactions to Getiier is really the same, namely, to spell out what is involved in the justification condition. It does not matter whether this spelling out consists in the addition of a fresh condition or in building up such a condition in the very definition of the term 'justification'. Clark, Chisholm and Hamlyn spell out by adding the fourth condition (iv) mentioned above. But Thalberg, Armstrong and Pollock make a certain condition an integral part of the very nature of justification. But the condition that they thus integrate into the nature of justification is not the same as the fourth condition mentioned above of Clark, Chisholm and Hamlyn. It is much stronger, namely.

(v) The statements(s) which S uses must be *known* to be true. Pollock and Armstrong rightly insist on this stronger requirement because condition (iv) is too weak and does not, contrary to its proponents' belief, provide any guarantee against counter examples. In fact, as Armstrong (1973 : 153) points out, even with the addition of (iv) it is possible to construct fresh counter examples, and this has indeed been done by Saunders and Champavat (1964 : 8-9).[4] In order to rule out altogether the possibility of counter examples it is necessary to make the requirement stronger as specified in (v), according to Pollock and Armstrong.

S 1.5 On the analogy of the first type of reaction, the statement (v) could have been set up as the condition (iv) to supplement (iii) in the traditional analysis. In that case the statement (v) would not have been part of the justification condition included in the classical analysis. This is merely a verbal matter and it does not really matter which alternative is adopted. I follow Pollock and Armstrong in integrating statement (v) into the justification condition of the classical analysis. Even though the statement (v) (which is a part of the justification condition) renders the construction of counter examples theoretically impossible, it must be noted that this condition gives rise to another, but no less important, difficulty. This difficulty is that the addition of condition (v) (instead of condition (iv) to the classical analysis of knowledge results in an infinite regress. In trying to understand what is involved in knowing a given statement p, we are forced to refer to a knowledge of another statement q. Now when the very nature of knowledge in general is in question, to explain one piece of knowledge in terms of another piece of knowlebge is only to push the question backwards unendingly instead of answering it. Any adequate analysis of knowledge in general must somehow remedy this situation. The remedy lies in distinguishing between two types of justification, namely, (a) justification of empirical statements and (b) justification of apriori statements,and to chatacteristerise these two types separately. This is what I do below.

S 1.6 (a) *Jusiification of empirical statements* : The justification of empirical statements will be in terms of other empirical statements. But the process of backward justification does not go on for ever. It is bound to terminate at a certain stage, namely, the stage where the justifying statements are themselves justified not by other statements but by direct experience. The statements that thus justified are the so called basic statements. These are simply reports of direct experiences[5] and they constitute the base of the system of all empirical statements. Every empirical statement has ultimateiy to be grounded in some sort of basic statements and such grounding constitutes the terminus for empirical justification. Such terminal justification may be called, following Popper (1968 : 94), non-prospositional (direct) and the justification of empirical statemedts in terms of other empirical statements may be called propositional (indirect).

(b) *Justification of apriori statements :* The problem of apriori justification is also similar. An apriori statements is one whose truth is independent of experience but this does not mean that it is self-justifying though some people like Ayer (1946 : 16) think so. Quite a large number of apriori statements need justification in terms of other apriori statements. But in this case also the process of back justification does come to an end when we reach fundamental or self-evident apriori statements. There are of course difficulties in deciding what is self-evident or fundamental. But by and large in relation to any system of beliefs there is no difficulty in at least roughly demarcating the area of self-evident statements.[6] And it is these that constitute the base of the system of apriori statements. And it is these that constitute the terminus for the justification of apriori statements. Here too as in the case of empirical statements the justification of self-evident propositions may be called non-propositional or direct. For justification of such propositions is in terms not of other propositions but of direct intuition (as against direct sense experience) about their truth. By stretching somewhat the propositional and non-propositional justification mentioned earlier in case of empirical statements, one may apply the distinction in the case of apriori statements also. The justification of self-evident propositions is called direct or non-propositional and the justification of apriori statements in terms of further apriori statements is propositional or indirect.

Notes and References

1. As noted before (fn 0.2), I deliberately abstain from equating 'pramā' with 'knowledge' to avoid anticipation.

2. tadvati tatprakārakoanubhavo yathārthaḥ. . .sa eva prametyucyate. "A cognition which has, for its subject, something which possesses the character which it (*i.e.*, the cognition) has for its predicate, is a valid cognition. . It is this (veridical non-mnemic cognition) which is called pramā (*i.e.*, right knowledge)." "TS 35" Translated by Bhattacharya 1975 : 7. Cf BP SBBS 1.1.4. See S 11.9.

3. Armstrong 1973:137; Quine and Ullian 1970:6; Quinton 1967:345-; Thalberg 1969:794. See also Hamlyn 1977:20-1; Chisholm 1077:102-4.

4. The counter example given by Saunders and Champavat is briefly as follows :

   Smith claims to know that Jones owns a Ford on the ground that (where p = Jones owns a Ford)

   (i) p is true,

   (ii) Smith believes that p;

   (iii) p is uttered by Brown who is reliable and honest.

   But Smith's claim does not amount to knowledge for Jones sells his Ford and wins another Ford in a raffle within an hour so that the truth of Brown's statement is merely a matter of coincidence.

5. Russell 1951a:139; Ayer 1946:10, 1977:67.

6. The question of self-evidence is much more complicated than indicated here. Similarly the question of the epistemological status of basic statements is much more involved; it leads to a consideration of the relation of illusory experience to basic statements. However, I have ignored these complications in the present context. For further details see Pollock 1974:25-32; Russel 1951a:137-49; Ayer 1977:51-68.

2

PRAMĀ AS KNOWLEDGE (I)

S 2.1 Now that the contemporary concept of knowledge is analysed, a yard-stick is available to understand and assess the Indian concept of pramā. Let me, therefore, return to this latter concept and elaborate upon it further. As noted before a familiar definition of pramā is that it is a cognition which corresponds to reality (fn 1.2). A component concept of this definition is *cognition* and calls for some explanation. There are different theories regarding what is a cognition; of these three may be mentioned here : (i) Quality theory (ii) Action theory and (iii) Substance theory. Let me explain in brief each one of them.

(i) *Quality theory* :

This theory is subscribed to by Naiyāyikas. According to the Nyāya system, soul is not intrinsically conscious but can become conscious under certain circumstances, consciousness is thus accidental to its nature; and cognition, because it involves awareness or consciousness, is said to be a quality of the self.[1]

I shall comment on this theory (and also) on the other two after stating them.

(ii) *Action theory* :

According to this theory a cognition is a process or an activity rather than a quality of the soul.[2] In the Indian tradition there is a distinction between quality and action[3] and the distinction is sometimes emphasised with scholastic zeal. In saying that cognition is a process, the question whether such a process it intrinsic to the self is left open. This view is generally ascribed to the Bhāṭṭa school of Pūrva-mīmāṃsā.

(iii) *Substance theory* :

This theory is advocated by Advaita-vedānta and holds that a cognition goes to constitute the very nature of the self.[4] This view contrasts sharply with Nyāya view according to which a cognition is external to the self. It also differs from the activity theory in that cognition is said to be the substratum and is not what inheres in a substance. A process or an activity can only inhere in a substratum but cannot itself form a substratum. This is also true of a quality. A quality like an action can only inhere in a substance but cannot be itself a substance.

S 2.2 These theories make a strange reading today and the only excuse in their favour is a pervading confusion between two different senses of cognition (jñāna), namely cognition as consciousness and cognition as what has come to be regarded after Frege, namely, a thought or a proposition. These two senses of cognition roughly correspond to the locutions "cognition of—" and "cognition that—". "Cognition of—" is used to express our cognitive experiences such as the cognition of a table, the cognition of a rope etc. But these experiences are simply psychological occurrences and cannot be said to be either true or false, whereas truth or falsity is a hall-mark of a proposition. It is to express a proposition that the locution "cognition that—". For example, the cognition that 'there are ten coins in my Pocket' is either true or false and so is the cognition $E=mc^2$. (The equation of Einstein, meaning energy equals mass times the square of velocity of light.) As it happens the second cognition is true.

In logical or epistemological inquiry it is the cognition in the sense of "cognition that—" that is in question and not the cognition in the sense of a cognitive experience or consciousness. In fact the question of consciousness is not even relevant in an epistemological understanding of cognition as a vehicle of truth or falsity. A cognition may not involve consciousness at all, though it may under certain circumstances. And even when it does involve consciousness, the consciousness so involved is irrelevant to its epistemological analysis. There are cognitions which are either true or false but which may not be contemplated either by me or by any others. And this fact does not in the least alter the character of cognition in question. In fact, people have gone to the extent of saying that cognitions are themselves entities, abstract ones, existing eternally and independently of the beings that may think, and express them. They are expressible in principle in human language but such an expression is theoretically not necessary to their nature. This view immediately reminds us of the Platonic world of Ideas but it is not merely a matter of antiquity, it has its champions even in recent times like Frege (1977 : 27) and Church (1956 : 26) and it has even been ascribed to Naiyāyikas as well (Mullatti 1977 : 21-57). But this is taking the matter into metaphysics instead of limiting oneself to epistemology. My concern here is epistemological rather than metaphysical and I am not particularly interested in the metaphysical views regarding the nature of a cognition. An epistemological analysis is consistent with more than one metaphysical views and does not presuppose any one of them.

S 2.3 Epistemologically a cognition is something either true or false. Is it then merely a sentence or a statement, that is, a linguistic entity of a certain sort, or is it some thing more ? Any attempt to make it non-linguistic involves serious difficulties and to say that it is just a linguistic entity is counter intuitive, though not necessarily wrong. In the Indian tradition including Nyāya and Advaita-vedānta thought there is a pervasive distinction between the (linguistic) expression of a language and what that expression expresses (Mullatti 1977 : 21; Matilal 1971 : 93). This distinction is not always explicitiy made but is always there in the background. A cognition, strictly speaking, is in the tradition, not a sentence but what it expresses, namely, a thought or a proposition And it is 'a thought' or 'a proposition' and not the sentence expressing it, is the vehicle of truth or falsity according to the Indian thinkers.

Pramā then is a cognition or cognitions understood in this sense *i.e.*, in the sense of the vehicle of truth value. Of course not any cognition but only true cognitions constitute pramā. But now the important question is whether any true cognitions counts as pramā or does it have to meet any further requirement to count as pramā. The familiar definition just referred to clearly suggests that a pramā is nothing more than a true cognition. This is made explicit by Annaṃbhaṭṭa (fn 1.2).

S 2.4 However, there are indications in Bhāṭṭa Mīmāṃsaka, and Advaita-vedānta literature to the effect that a further requirement is to be fulfilled by a cognition before it can count as pramā. This is the requirement of novelty. If a cognition is to be pramā, it must not only be true but also new according to their indications.[5] This view is also held by several modern Indian expositors of Advaita-vedānta. For example, D.M. Datta (1972 : 20) says "Pramā is generally defined as a cognition having the twofold characteristic of truth and novelty . . ." Again Hiriyanna (1975 : 36) says that the novelty (anadhigatatva) is also an indispensable requirement of pramā. But what is surprising is that an eminent Nyāya expositor like Athalye (1974 : 177,185) also holds a similar view. He says :

> The author defines anubhava as 'all knowledge other than rememberance,' *i.e.*, all cognitions which are newly acquired and are not repetitions of former ones. . . The Naiyāyikas restrict all proofs to anubhava or new cognitions and call smṛti mere repetitions thereof caused by saṅskāra from previous impressions.

The consideration that which prompts these modern Indian thinkers to hold that novelty is a requirement of knowledge is, I think, basically that memory is not a source of pramā. In fact, 'jñāna' (which I have rendered as cognition) is usually divided in the Indian tradition into anubhava (anubhūti) and smṛti. And it is yathārthānubhava to the exclusion of yatharthasmṛti that is treated as pramā.[6]

S 2.5 This would suggests that my talk above of pramā as if it were true cognition (yathārthajñāna) is, strictly speaking, not faithful to the text; the term anubhava (aoubhūti) is narrower in scope than jñāna and yet I have used them interchangeably by rendering the two as cognitions. I should have rendered 'anubhava' by another English term of correspondingly narrower scope, my excuse for not having done so is that whatever difference there is between jñāna and anubhūti, is of marginal epistemological importance, especially because the criterion of truth for both anubhava and smṛti is ultimately the same according to the texts.[7]

Further, I think it is desirable to leave open the question whether or not memory is a source of pramā. There has been a controversy on this question even amongst contemporary thinkers, for example, while Hamlyn (1977 : 214) holds that memory is not a source of knowledge, Pollock (1974 : 199) sees little reason in not regarding it as such a source. But this controversy is not relevant to my purpose here, since the question whether memory is a source of pramā is really independent of the question, whether novelty is a requirement or condition of knowledge. Even if one grants with Naiyāyikas and Mīmāṃsaka (and Advaitins) (S 2.4) that memory is to be excluded from pramā their equation of novelty with such exclusion cannot be accepted for there is a sense in which even yathārthānubhava (or simply anubhava for that matter) can be said to be not new. For example, I may perceive now that this table is brown as I have done on several days in the past. So my present perceptual cognition cannot be said to be new merely because it happens to be different from memory.[8] If, therefore, novelty is to be made a requirement of pramā it has to be first separated from smṛti. There seems to be no textual evidence that this has been done. Hence, it will not be correct to say that in the Indian tradition novelty is made a condition of pramā though it is correct to say that memory is excluded from pramā. It is especially incorrect to say as Athalye does, that for the Naiyāyikas novelty is a condition of pramā.

S 2.6 The belief condition dealt with earlier course has no implication regarding novelty. Even if novelty were made a condition of knowledge (not pramā), it will have to be an additional and independent condition. In other words, a cognition that goes to constitute pramā may or may not be new. Similarly a cognition that is believed in may or may not be new. Even if a cognition is both new and believed in, it is still an open question whether it would count as pramā. It is, therefore, relevant to ask whether the belief condition as distinct from the novelty condition is involved in pramā.

S 2.7 There is no *explicit* textual evidence, as far as I know, for saying that in the Indian tradition in general and in Nyāya and Advaita in particular, belief was made a necessary condition of pramā. Lack of explicit evidence of course does not warrant the opposite conclusion, namely, that belief was not made a condition of pramā. Since the question of the relevance of belief condition was never consciously raised in the Indian tradition, the only thing left for an interpreter is to go by indirect evidence and general considerations. The indirect evidence is the obvious recognition in the Indian tradition that pramā, in so far as it belongs to humans, is imperfect at least in the sense that it is incomplete. There are more things in the universe than those the human mind ever thought of.[9] This obviously means there are more truths than are embraced in pramā. And this by implication means that pramā cannot be the same as true cognition. This goes directly against the explicit evidence cited above (fn 1.2). The conflict between the direct and the indirect evidence, it is obvious, can only be resolved in favour of indirect evidence lest human beings be considered as omniscient. Pramā, then, has even in the Indian tradition, at least by implication if not explicity, a further or condition or conditions other than truth condition. The problem is to decide how many these further conditions are, and whether they include the belief condition. As just noted there is no explicit evidence for saying that the belief condition was explicity accepted. Nor is there explicit evidence for saying that it was explicitly rejected. But this time we have our clue in a general consideration which favours this belief condition and which of course would be readily accepted by the traditional Indian thinkers. This general consideration is that it would be logically absurd for a person to lay claim to knowledge and yet disown belief, that 'S knows that p' is incompatible with 'S does not believe that p'. Of course, there is a distinction, beginning even from Plato or earlier, between *knowledge* and (true) *belief*; it is obvious that *knowledge* is not the same as belief since a belief may be true or false, whereas, as already noticed, (S 1.3) what is known must be necessarily true. But as clearly shown, not every true belief can count as knowledge. But this distinction between knowledge and belief does not come in the way of the two being also related in some other way, and the relation is that if 'a person S knows that p', then it follows that 'S also believes that p', and this general consideration regarding the relation between the two knowledge and belief is so fundamental and intuitive that there is no reason to believe that it was not acceptable to the Indian thinkers. This means that the Indian thinkers would also accept the belief condition as a necessary condition of pramā.

S 2.8 Now one might object to my borrowing support for the belief condition of pramā from the contemporary analysis of concept of knowledge, where one is assessing the concept of pramā itself in the light of the concept of knowledge, how can one argue that pramā has a certain characteristic *on the ground that* knowledge also has it. Any support for the belief condition for pramā must come not from an analysis of concept of knowledge but from different quarters. This would indeed be a plausible objection if I were indeed borrowing support from concept of knowledge.

Despite appearances to the contrary and as remarked above, I am appealing not to the concept of knowledge but to general and fundamental intuition with which every one agres and there is no reason why the traditional Indian thinkers would not agree. It just happens that the general consideration is also a part of the analysis of the concept of pramā but it derives its strength from its own nature and not from its being involved in the analysis of the concept of knowledge. So my procedure in saying that the belief condition is necessarily involved in the concept of pramā as it is in the concept of knowledge is not really open to the objection in question.

S 2.9 It is thus seen that pramā shares two characteristics of knowledge, namely, truth and belief. Does it share also the third characteristic of knowledge, namely, the justification condition? Here again the answer is not easy; there is no explicit evidence on which one could base the answer. The answer has got to be reconstructed from circumstantial evidence. I will begin the reconstruction by noting that pramā as conceived above is said to be of different types. According to the Nyāya system it is of four types, namely, perceptual (pratyakṣa), inferential (anumiti), identificational (upamiti) and testimonial (śābda),[10] to these Advaita-vedānta adds two more kinds *viz.*, postulational (arthāpatti) and absential (anupalabdhi) (Vp 8).

A brief account of these different kinds is given below (SS 2.10-15; SS 3.1-26). I request the reader to refer to these pages before proceeding further. A reference to these different types even at this stage is necessary because my reconstruction of my answer regarding the justification in relation to pramā depends on the distinction between them. The point I wish to make is that each type of pramā satisfies the justification condition; therefore pramā as such also satisfies it.

S 2.10 Let me consider pratyakṣa pramā first. Both the Naiyāyikas and Advaita-vedāntins distinguish different kinds of pratyakṣa pramā. But inspite of their distinctions the most central and crucial fact about this kind is that it is at the very least a direct cognition that is true, and we have just seen above that it is also a cognition believed in. What kind of justification, if at all, can this kind of pramā have; as pointed out earlier in the case of basic statements the justification is terminal *i.e.*, it is justified by direct experience and pratyakṣa pramā consists either of such basic statements (if it is laukika, or mundane) or of statements which are also equally direct though these cannot be self-evident as I have used the term (S 1.6). I have used the term justification to cover only empirical and apriori statement and it would not, therefore, be applicable, strictly speaking, to pratyakṣa pramā of alaukika variety.[11] But if I am permitted to make use of the analogy of pratyakṣa pramā of the laukika variety, then it seems plausible to talk of justification, even of pratyakṣa pramā of the alaukika variety, in a similar fashion for, the most distinctive character of both kinds of pratyakṣa pramā are that they consist of direct cognitions and; an obvious implication of my account of justification (S 1.6) is that the justification of a direct cognition (empirical, apriori or otherwise) is terminal. In other words, these are all self-justifying basically in the same sense. So then it seems plausible to say that both the traditional Indian thinkers, if they were made conscious of the problem, would say pratyakṣa pramā in all of its varieties (except the nirvikalpaka variety (fn 2.11) satisfy the jurisfication condition as well in addition to two condition already noted, namely, truth condition and belief condition. I am encouraged to say this because there is nothing in the text either directly or indirectly which goes against what I have said, and also because it brings out what is best, implicity, or explicitly, in the substance of traditional Indian thought systems, especially, in Nyāya and Advaita. It would relate the traditional Indian thinker to the contemporary idiom in a more desirable fashion.

S 2.11 Anumiti :—This is another very important kind of pramā recognised in most traditional Indian schools including Nyāya and Advaita-vedānta. Though they differ in varying degrees in their account of anumāna (inference)—especially regarding the number of its elements, all these schools (except Cārvāka) agree in saying that it is a pramāṇa and is the instrumental cause of anumiti. Curiously enough none of the schools discusses the question of formal validity of anumāna and the fallacies that are discussed are all material. All schools, (except Cārvāka which does not recognise inference) seem to take formal validity of an inference for granted. What is more all schools (except Cārvākas) take it for granted that the elements of inference are true. This is seen from the fact that every example of inference in every school (excepting Cārvāka) consists of true elements. There is not even the slightest indication of the possibility of a valid inference with some or all elements being false. In other words anumāna is necessarily what some contemporary logicians, for example Copi (1972 : 23) call, a sound inference *i.e.*, an inference which is formally valid and whose elements are true.

Basically justification consists in adducing good grounds for a given prosposition. In this sense the conclusion of an inference is justified in terms of its premisses, whether the inference is deductive or inductive. If the inference is deductive the justification is especially satisfactory.[12] But this is so only if premisses are true (in addition of course the inference being formally valid). For as remarked above, it is possible that in a valid inference the conclusion may be true and yet all or some of the premisses may be false. In such a case the premisses cannot be said to provide good grounds for the conclusion, in an epistemological context. (In a logical context of course even false premisses are said to provide good grouds for the conclusion provided the inference in question is valid). Thus, so far as this second form of pramā is concerned, there is the guarantee that statement (iv) to the effect that the justifying statemente must be true, is satisfied. But, as noted earlier, this is not enough for *pramā* to count as knowledge. So the question that must be answered is really not whether *pramā* satisfies statement (iv) but whether it satisfies statement (v) (which says that the justifying statements must be known to be true). How is this latter question to be answered ?

S 2.12 In the case of pratyakṣa pramā this question does not arise because there justification is direct and terminal and not in terms of further statements. But it does arise in all its force in the present case—the case of anumiti pramā. Perhaps a clue is to be found in Nyāya-bhāṣya. Vātsyāyana says in these sūtras that inference consists of five elements, namely, thesis (pratijñā), reason (hetu), example (udāharaṇa), application (upanaya) and conclusion (nigamana). Of these last is the conclusion (anumiti) and the first is a provisional assertion of the conclusion, the other three constitute what may be called the premisses of the conclusion. The four elements other than anumiti are correlated with the four pramāṇas, that Vātsyāyana recognises, namely, pratyakṣa (perception), anumāna (inference), upamāna (identification), and śabdā (testimony).[13]

Thesis (pratijñā) : The pratijñā is said to be the result of testimony ; hetu is said to be the result of anumāna ; udāharaṇa and upanaya, are respectively the outcome of pratyakṣa and upamāna. Before these sūtras are taken as possible source of answer to the question raised at the end of the last para, several difficulties that arise are to be sorted out. First of all, it is not at all clear how pratijñā is the outcome of testimony for, if it were indeed such, *i.e.*, the product of testimony, it would be pramā by its own right and there would be no further need of its being derived as a conclusion also. And it will no longer have provisional status that it is supposed to have as a member of inference. This question has not been faced explicitly by the Naiyāyikas. But the Nyāya epistemology allows the situation represented by the question. For it seems to be taken for granted by the Naiyāyikas that the independence of the pramāṇas does not come in their way of their convergence, in other words, one and the same object can be known by different pramāṇas ; even when a certain object is known by one pramāṇa to be doubly sure of his knowledge. This explanation seems to be corroborated by the view that pramāṇas are also means of scrutiny.[14]

But all this based on the supposition that pratijñā is the result of testimony. But the supposition itself may be questioned for it is not at all clear which authority is the basis of it. In fact, in so far as pratijñā is the proposition at issue there does not seem to be any authority behind it and so it does not carry conviction to say that pratijñā is the result of testimony.

Reason (hetu) : The second element of inference according to Vātsyāyana is hetu. But his version of hetu[15] is far different from the Navya-nyāya (and the Advaita) version.[16] According to Vātsyayāna hetu consists of a conjunction of roughly of the syllogistic minor premises and the syllogistis major premises[17] (Potter 1977 : 245) and this whole conjunction is held to be known by inference. It is rather puzzling why Vātsyāyana clubs the two premisses into one and why he claims that the whole conjunction is known by inference. For it is obvious that the syllogistic minor premiss ('The hill has smoke') can also be known by perception. In fact, it is usually known by perception and rarely by inference. Similarly the syllogistic major which constitutes the second conjunct ('Whatever has smoke has fire') cannot be said to be known by inference. In fact, as far as I know neither in Vātsyayāna nor in any later literature is any indication of an inference with a universal statement as conclusion. So I simply fail to make sense of Vātsyāyana's claim that hetu is known by anumāna. And besides there is further difficulty that if hetu (or for that matter any other element) is known by inference, there will be an infinite regress. The given inference would involve a second inference in the establishment of its hetu and the second inference would again involve third inference in the establishment of its own hetu and so on ad infinitum. And the question with which we started, namely whether anumiti pramā satisfies the statement (v) will not have been answered.

Example (*udāharaṇa*) : Vātsyāyana also claims that udāharaṇa is known by perception. He seems to say this because his conception of udāharaṇa is also at variance with that of Navya-nyāya and Advaita.vedānta. According to him udaharaṇa just consists of either a negative or a positive instance. And what the Navyanyāya and Advaita designate by the word 'udāharaṇa' namely, the universal concomitance is seen above transferred by Vātsyāyana, to hetu. Given these circumstances Vātsyāyana's claim that udāharaṇa is known by perception seems to be plausible but udāharaṇa as it is conceived in Navya-nyāya and Advaita—vedānta in the sense of universal concomitance can hardly be said to be known by perception alone in the usual sense of that term.[18]

Application (*upanaya*) : Upanaya on Vātsyāyana's view is known by upamāna (identification) (fn 2.13). But Vātsyāyana's conception of upanaya is also different from that of Navya-nyāya and Advaita-vedānta and the difference is a consequence of his conception of udāharaṇa. As noted above udāharaṇa according to Vātsyāyana consists of just instances either positive or negative. Upanaya consists in asserting either that the subject of the inference is similar to the instance cited in udāharaṇa or that it is different from the instance. If the instance cited in udāharaṇa is positive, and, therefore, upanaya also is positive, it would be plausible to say that upanaya is known through upamāna.[19] For upanaya according to Vātsyāpana and also Navya-nyāya consists in identifying an object on the basis of its known similarity with something else (NBh 1.1.38 ; TS 58). But if the instance cited in udāharaṇa is negative and, hence, the upanaya also is negative, it is difficult to see how the upanaya in question is known by upamāna. For there is no similarly involved between the instance cited and subject of the inference. [But see Siddhānta-candrodaya cited in Athalye (1974 : 328)]. But this view of upanaya is shared by Vātsyāyana (as also Gautama NS 1.1.38). It is not accepted by Navya-nyāya and Advaita-vedānta. According to these schools upanaya is what hetu is according to Vātsyāyana, namely, a conjunction of the syllogistic minor and syllogistic major. Another word for it is parāmarśa (consideration) (fn 2.17). On this latter view of upanaya the claim that the upanaya is known by upamāna would of course be untenable. For the notion of similarity plays no role either in the syllogistic minor ('The hill has smoke') or syllogistic major ('Whatever has smoke, has fire).

S 2.13 These various considerations show that Vātsyāyana's attempt to correlate the four elements (other than nigamana or conclusion) with the four pramāṇas recognised by Nyāya system will not do. One may suggest that the attempt confuses the general question, namely, how the four elements of an inference are established with the specific question, whether the elements of a given inference are as a matter of fact true. The first is an epistemological question and the second is a logical question. And the answers to the two would be accordingly different. A statement may be true or false without being known to be such. What the Nyāya theory of inference requires is that the elements should be true not that they are known to be true. The point of suggestion may be brought out with referenec to the following example.

1. This cow has hooves,
2. Because it has horns,
3. Whatever, has horns has hooves, for example a bull,
4. This is so,

∴ 5. It is so.

This example is valid because its elements are true without worrying about how their truth is known. But such a suggestion would be unfair not only to Vātsyāyana but to Indian tradition in general. For the whole point of Vatsyayana's attempt is to emphasise the epistemological aspect of inference, *i.e.*, elements of an inference must be known to be true not just be true. This will be brought out more clearly below. (S 2.15).

S 2.14 The Advaitins recognise only three elements in an inference and hold that either the first three or the last three elements of the five membered syllogism of the Navya-naiyāikas are by themselves sufficient ; and that the remaining two elements are absolutely superfluous (VP 75-6). They also recognise six pramāṇas (VP 8) apparently, therefore, neither one to one correlation between the elements of an inference and the pramāṇas is possible in their case ; nor do they attempt such a correlation. But it would be interesting to notice the further awkward consequences which follow if we try to apply it to the three membered syllogism of the Advaitins. *First* : Vātsyāyana's claim that pratijñā is known by testimony will have to be rejected by Vedāntins even if only the first three elements of the pancāvayava vākya are admitted by Advaitins, for in that case pratijñā would really be identical with the conclusion and will have to be known by inference and not by testimony. The alternative would be to hold that one and the same element (namely, the conclusion) is known by both testimony and inference which, if not absurd, is at least unintended. *Second* : For the Advaitins hetu is the same as upanaya and, if according to Vātsyāyana upanaya is known by upamāna, hetu has also got to be similarly known which goes contrary to Vātsyāna's view. If Vātsyāyana's is to be preserved anumāna and upamāna would coalesce in the case of Advaitins. Further the Advaitins would simply reject Vātsyāyana's claim that his version of hetu is known by inference. They would hold that out of the two conjuncts of Vātsyāyana's version of hetu only the first is properly so called and the second is to be called udāharaṇa and the first would be for them known by pratyakṣa and the second inductively. In all this Advaitins are in agreement with Navya-naiyāyikas.[20]

It is thus seen that Vātsyāyana's attempt at a correlation of the elements of inference with the different pramāṇas fails very miserably but this does not mean that the different correlation is possible, which would avoid all the objections raised above and which would otherwise be satisfactory in every respect. No such correlation is possible and any attempt at correlation is misguided attempt and is altogether misleading in its effect.

S 2.15. What happens then to the question with which I started whether anumiti pramā satisfies the statement (v), namely, the justifying statements must be known to be true. I have tried to show that answer to this question in terms of Vātsyāyana's correlation is not tenable. Nevertheless a positive answer can, I think, be given in terms of the spirit of the Indian tradition as a whole in this regard. The important consideration to be remembered in this regard is that all the elements of an inference are to be true, How is this consideration to be satisfied. The person who uses anumāna as a means of pramā must satisfy himself that the elements are all true and this satisfaction does not mean just the subjective satisfaction of somehow believing that they are true. It is a satisfaction of logical type. It means either they are accepted on the ground of an expert authority or as a result of one's own investigations. The person who uses inference takes care that the elements are known to bc true, for, otherwise, it is impossible for him to ensure the condition that the elements are to be true. Of course if the expert authority is itself called in question then it has to yield to personal investigation, and even when personal investigation regards that truth of elements is also in doubt, there is a possibility of infinite regress. But this regress will be terminated when the investigation ends with direct experiences as happens if the elements are empirical in character ; or with self-evident statements as happens when the elements espeeially vyāpti, are apriori in character. These two possibilities have already been considered when thc nature of justification was discussed above (S 1.6). All this amounts to saying that any one who uses anumāna as a means of pramā satisfies himself that the elements other than anumiti are well grounded. This amounts to saying that these elements are known to be true. Since these elements jointly servc as justification for anumiti this means that in the case of anumiti also justifying statements are not only true but are knowu to be true,

So in the case of anumiti also the statement (v), namely, 'statements must be known to be true' is satisfied. It now remains to be seen whether the remaining types of pramā also satisfy the statement (v).

Notes and References

1. buddhyādayoaṣṭāvātmamātraviśeṣaguṇāḥ. "The eight qualities, cognition etc. are special attributes of soul only." TS 73. Translated by Athalye and Bodas 1974:361. Cf BP 51; NBH 2.2.24.

2. jñānakriyā hi sakarmikā. Pārthasārathi (śāstra-dīpikā) cited in Chatterjee 1939:12.

3. atha drvyāśritā jñeyā nirguṇā niṣkriyā guṇāḥ. "The qualities should be known as a biding in substances, and being without qualities and actions." BP 86. Translated by Madhavananda 1977:177. Cf TD 4.

4. . . . dravyātmakatā guṇasya. ". . . the quality is one with the substanee." SBBS 2.2.17. Translated by Gambhirananda 1972;397. See Satprakasananda 1974:89: Devaraja 1972 : 90.

5. pramā cājñātatavārthajñānamevātra. . . ajñātapadenātra jñātaviṣayoḥ smṛtyanuvādayorṇirāsaḥ. "Valid knowledge is the knowledge of an unknown real object . . . Here by the word 'unknown', there is the exclusion of recollection and restatement, which have known objects." MN 1-2. Translated by Raja, and Sastri 1975:2.

   But Advaita view of pramā is ambiguous: novelty is a property of pramā and memory cognition devoid of novelty could be accomodated under pramā. See VP 4-5.

6. sarvavyavahāraheturguṇobnddhirjñānam. sā dvividhā smṛtiranubhavaśca. saṃskāramātrajanyaṃ jñānaṃ smṛtiḥ. tadbhinnaṃ jñānamanubhavaḥ. sa dvividho yathārthoayathārthaśca. "Buddhi (*i.e.*, knowledge) is a quality which is a cause of all employment of words, and is the same as jñāna. It is of two kinds: mnemic knowledge and non-mnemic knowledge. Mnemic knowledge is that kind of knowledge which is solely caused by saṁskāra. Knowledge which is different from that (*i.e.*, from mnemic knowledge) is non-mnemic cognition. This is of two kinds; veridical and non-veridical TS 34-5. Translated by Bhattacharya 1975:.71. Cf. BP . 51

7. smṛtirapi dvividhā. yathārthāyathārthā ca. pramājanyā yathārthā. apramājanyāyathārtha. "Memory knowledge, too, is of two kinds, namely, valid and invalid. That (memory knowledge) which is caused by valid non-mnemic knowledge is valid. The (memory knowledge) which is caused by invalid (non-mnemic) knowledge is invalid." TS 65. Translated by Bhattacharya 1975:261.

8. Pollack (1974:198-99) in arguing for memory as a source of knowledge says that memory *can be* a source of *new* knowledge. Even if what he says were true, it is far from saying that novelty is a condition of knowledge.

9. jñānadhikaraṇamātmā sa dvividaḥ paramātmā jīvātmā ca. tatreśvaraḥ sarvajnaḥparamātmaika eva.

"The Soul is the substratum of knowledge. He is two fold, Human and Supreme. Of these the Supreme soul . . . is omniscient." TS 17. Translated by Athalye 1974:134.

jñānājñāṇā sukhitvādibhirjīvānām bhedasiddhau sutarāmīśvara bhedhaḥ. ' Since these souls, on account of their (varying) knowledge or ignorance, happiness or misery, etc. are proved to be different from one another they are more palpably different from God." SM 48. Tranlated by Madaavananda 1977:72.

10. yathārthanubhavascaturvidhaḥ pratyakṣānumityupamiti śābdabhedhāt. "Right apprehension (which is not mnemic) is of four kinds on account of the distinction between perceptual, inferential, analogical and verbal apprehensions.'' TS 36, Translated by Bhattacharya 1975:17. Cf BP 51-2.

11. The notion of indeterminate pratyakṣa is rather unclear, it is often said to be non-qualificational, hence, non-propositional.

12. Anumāna in the Indian contexts is thus deductive inference, inductive inference is not recognised as a pramāṇa and the status of inductive knowledge is left dubious. This has to be kept in mind in considering my account of the relationship between pramā and knowledge.

13. tasya pañcāvayavāḥ pratijñādayaḥ samūhamapekṣyāvayavā ucyante. teṣu pramāṇasamavāyaḥ. āgamaḥ pratijñā. heturanumānam. udāharaṇam pratyakṣam. upanyamupamānam. "and these five taken collectively are what have been called 'factors' (the seventh category), all the 'means of cognition' (or forms of valid cognition) are found to be present among these 'factors'; for instance, the 'statement of the conclusion' is verbal; the the statement of the probans' is inferential; the 'statement of the instance' is perceptual; 'the statement of the minor premiss' is analogical." NBH 1.1.1. Translated by Jha 1939:9.

14. pramāñairarthaparīkṣṇam nyāyaḥ. NBh 1.1.1. Cf Hiriyanna 1977:66, 69.

15. In Vātsyāyana's example about sound and non-eternality, the hetu consists of 'The sound is a product, and whetever is a product is non-eternal', (tasya sādhanatāvacanam hetuh. utpattidharmakatvāditi. utpattidharmakamanityam. . NBh 1.1.34).

16. dhūmavatvāditi hetuḥ. "On account of its possessing smoke—this is the reason." Translated by Bhattacharya 1975:86. See VP 75-6.

17. In standard example about smoke and fire the hetu according to Vātsyāyana is 'The hill has smoke and whatever has smoke has fire'. This in fact what latter in Navyanyāya came to be called parāmarśa or vyāpti-viśiṣṭa-pakṣa dharmatā-jñāna, pakṣa-dharmatā-jñāna alone being expressed by hetu.

vyāptiviśiṣṭakakśadharmatājñānam parāmarśah "Parāmarśa is the know-that a concomitant of the probandum (vyāptiviśiṣta) is a character of the subject of the conclusion." TS 44, Translated by Bhattacharya 1975:56-7, Cf BP, 68,

18. There is the unusual sense of perception (pratyakṣa) of the Naiyāyikas, namely, alaukika pratyakṣa according to them it is of three forms : (i) Sāmānya-lakṣana-pratyāsatti (intuition of universals), (ii) Jñāna-lakṣaṇa-pratyāsatti and (iii) Yogaja-pratyāsatti. Of these (i) is supposed to be employed in the apprehension of the universal statements that the Naiyāyikas are obviously wrong holding this view is conclusively shown by Mullatti 1977:83-4.

19. The Advaita conception of upamāna is somewhat different from that of Nyāya as is pointed out below (SS 3.1-3).

20. In claiming that an inference consists either the first three or the last three of the pañcāvayava vākya the Advaitins are differing substantially from the Navya-naiyāyikas. For the Navya-naiyāyikas the hetu and upanaya differ from each other, upanaya being a conjunction of hetu and udāha- But for the Advaitins upanaya is the same as hetu.

3

PRAMĀ AS KNOWLEDGE (II)

S 3.1. Identificational pramā (upamiti) :—Upamāna according to Nyāya, as remarked in Chapter II, consists in identifying an object on the basis of some known similarity. Even though most Indian schools recognise upamāna as an independent pramāṇa, a little reflection will show that it really reduces itself to inference in its Nyāya version. In its Nyāya version upamāna involves four factors :

(1) A person's first hand experience (perception) of an object A at an earlier point of time,

(ii) The perceived similarity of another object B to the already known object A,

(iii) The knowledge that whatever is similar to an A is a B,

and (iv) The identification of B at a later point of time on the basis of (i), (ii), and (iii).[1]

Now what is the source for the general similarity between B and A ? According to Nyāya it is testimony. But if so, all that we have in upamāna is an inference whose premisses are based either on perception or on testimony, and upamāna altogether loses its autonomy. This result follows whether or not testimony is itself an independent pramāṇa (see SS 8.6—8).

S 3.2. The Naiyāyikas talk about identification as consisting in the saṅjñā, saṅjñi relation, *i.e.*, the relation between a sign and the thing signified ; the saṅjñā being the word 'gavaya' and saṅjñi being the animal gavaya. But what sign or word signifies what thing is a mere matter of convention and is not an epistemological question. This is indeed acknowledged by the Navya-naiyāyikas themselves.[2] The issue discussed under upamāna is really the identification of an unknown object. The process by which such identifi- is made is independent of a given language and its system of signs, and is truly epistemologically insignificant. It is after all a process of acquiring a certain sort of knowledge. The identification of an object which was not known before is a matter of classifica tion. And when an unknown object is assigned to a class, it means that within a given language the class-name in question comes to be applied to the unknown object thus classified. In acquiring the new (class) name the object in question has come to establish a certain relation with the name. And this may indeed be called the saṅjña-saṅjñi relation in a certain sense. But firstly there is the danger that when we talk of the relation of a word to its referrent, the referrent need not be an object hitherto unknown ; *i.e.*, the question of identification may not have been involved. Secondly there is also the danger that in talking of the saṅjña-saṅjñi relation we may be tying ourselves to a particular word and its referent in a given language, and thus get bogged down in purely linguistic (and hence empirical) issues as against philosophical ones. The Naiyāyikas are really concerned with philosophical issues in this context and not linguistic ones.

S 3.3. It is interesting to note that the Advaita conception of upamāna is very significantly different from the Nyāya conception. According to the Advaitins, upamāna is a means of knowing the similarity of an object perceived at an earlier moment with an object perceived at a later moment on the basis of the observed similarity of the latter with the former.[3]

The Advaita conception of upamana can be formalised as :

$$(U_1) \qquad Lgc$$
$$\therefore \qquad Lcg$$

(Lxy=x is like y ; c=my cow ; g=the gavaya I now see). U^1 is enthymematic since a premiss is taken for granted. This premiss which concerns the symmetrical character of the binary relation Lxy is : (x)(y)(Lxy—Lyx). Once this premise is added to U_1, a formal proof of validity can easily be constructed for the inference in question.

The Nyāya conception of upamāna can be symbolised as follows :

$$
\begin{array}{ll}
(U_2) & (x)(y)[(Cx.\ Lyx) \rightarrow Gy] \\
 & Cc.Lgc \\
\therefore & Gg
\end{array}
$$

(Lxy=x is like y ; Cx=x s a cow ; Gy=x is a gavaya ; c=my cow ; g=the strange animal is that I now see). U_2 is valld as it stands, and a formal proof for its validity can easily be constructed. Even though the difference between U_1 and U_2 is significant and obvious, yet a little reflection on U_1 shows that, the Advaita conception lacks autonomy just as the Nyāya conception does. In the case of Advaita also upamāna reduces itself to inference. The only premiss in U_1, is perceptual and the missing premiss concerning symmetry is perhaps based on testimony. But the sources of premisses do not matter. What matters is that U_1 is an inference and in reducing to U_1 the Advaita version of upamāna iooses its claim to independence. Because of this reduction, the question (the modified version of the justification condition, see SS 1.4-5), whether upamiti satisfies the statement (v) reduces itself to the question whether anumiti does so. Since I have already answsred this latter question in the affirmative (SS 2.11-15), I conclude that upamiti also satisfies the statement (v).

S 3.4. Testimonial pramā (śābda pramā) :—Śābda pramā is another type recognised by most Indian schools only exceptions being the Buddhist, the Cārvāka, and the Vaiśeṣika systems. In essentials the Nyāya account and Advaita account of śābda pramā are in agreement, according to whom it is a true sentence uttered or obtained from a trustworthy source.[4] Both distinguish two kinds of śābda pramā, laukika and alaukika. Laukika śābda pramā is obtained through the words of trustworthy human beings whereas alaukika śābda is acquired through the scriptures. Of course the two systems differ with respect to the authorship of scriptures. The Nyāya holds that God is the author of the scriptures and that the authorship is pauruṣeya. The Advaitins, on the other hand, claim that the scriptures are authorless (apauruṣeya). But the question of of authorship of the scripture is unimportant, in this epistemological context ; what is important is that there are these two kinds of śābda pramā. A detailed discussion of the logical character of śabda pramāṇa which corresponds to this kind of pramā is given in later Chapters VI-XI. For the time being this extremely brief formulation of the traditianal view will suffice.

Let me raise the question whether the śābda-pramā satisfies the condition expressed by the statement (v). So far as the laukika variety of śābda-pramā is concerned, the answer is clear enough ; it does satisfy the justification condition. A little reflection will suffice to show that laukika śābda pramā reduces itself either to pratyakṣa-pramā or to anumiti. And I have already shown above that in the case of either type of pramā the justification condition is satisfied. Any statement coming from trustworthy person is based on his own experience or reasoning and if I have leisure, the ability and the motivation to conduct similar observations and reasonings, I would have no need of the statement from such a trustworthy person, and one often either restates or replaces testimonial statements by personal investigations, and this personal investigation is necessarily of two types, namely, sensuous and rational (based on reason).

S 3.5. But, however, the primary motivation for recognition of śābda as a distinct pramā and śabda-pramāṇa as distinct pramāṇa comes from the desire to uphold the inviolability of the scriptures. It is, therefore, alaukika śābda that acquires a special importance and it is with reference to this kind of śābda pramā that the question with regard to the justification has got to be answered. Is the justification condition satisfied by this variety of śābda-pramā ? To answer this question, I have only to recall what I have said earlier about terminal justification (S 1.6), in substance a justification is said to be terminal if it calls for no further justification. It is because of this reason I described the justification involved in pratyakṣa pramā as terminal. In the case of anumiti, the justification is not immediately terminal but eventually terminal in the sense that the regress of process of justification eventually comes to a halt when we reach basic statements or self-evident statements. Now by the very definition of alaukika-śābda, the scriptural statements are self justifying and admit of no further justification. In this sense alaukika ṣābda may be said to satisfy the justification condition. But if this is so, how is one to classify scriptural statements ? They are surely not basic statements in the technical sense defined earlier, nor are they reducible to basic statements. But according to my own account of the nature of justification (S 1.6) there are only two types of statements that terminate the process of justification—basic statements in case of empirical statements in general and self-evident apriori propositions in apriori statements in general. Scriptural statements being neither empirical nor apriori would seem to go beyond the scope of justification as conceived by me, and this is indeed so while I personally hesitate to classify scriptural statements as self-evident (for obviously they are not empirical). The traditional Indians seem to have classified them as either self-evident or as reducible to self-evident statements. There is no other way of understanding their admission of alaukikas-śābda. For them the scriptural statements are either eternal or near eternal (*i.e.*, of divine origin). They express eternal truths just as apriori statements do, and stand on the same footing as apriori statements, so far as their epistemological status is concerned. If my understanding of the logical character of scriptural statements is correct, there are only two possibilities in the case of alaukika-śābda pramā :

(i) a given scriptural statement is itself self-evident, hence, calls for no further justification, in other words, it is self justifying and is terminus of all scriptural justifications. These include the so called revealed truths also.

(ii) a given scriptural statement may be justified in terms of other scriptural statements and this process of backward justification may go on until certain self-evident statements are reached which put an end to the need for further justification. It is obvious that in either of these two possibilities justification condition is satisfied. Given that the laukika variety of śābda-pramā also meets the justification condition just noted above, it follows that śābda pramā as a whole can be taken to conform to justification condition.

S 3.6. Postulational pramā (arthāpatti-pramā) :—This kind of pramā is recognised by Mīmāṃsakas and Vedāntins only. It consists in postulating a cognition in order to resolve an apparent conflict between two cognitions already known to be true. One of the stock examples of this kind of pramā is that Devadatta must be eating by night (since he is fat and does not eat by day), that Devadatta must be eating by night is accordingly postulated to account for the apparent conflict between cognitions that he is fat and that he does not eat by day[5] ; these apparently conflicting cognitions being already known to be true. The corresponding pramāṇa for arthāpatti pramā is arthāpatti. The distinction between arthāpatti as pramā andarthāpatti-pramāṇa is analogous to anumāna and anumiti. As already seen anumiti is the conclusion of anumāna. Similarly arthāpatti as pramā is the conclusion of arthāpatti-pramāṇa. And arthāpatti-pramāṇa itself consists of three cognitions including arthāpatti pramā. In the case of stock example mentioned a few lines earlier arthāpatti pramāṇa is :

1. Devadatta is fat,
2. Devadatta does not eat by day,

∴ 3. Devadatta must be eating by night.

In this example only the last cognition counts as arthāpatti-pramā.

The Advaitins (and Mīmāṃsakas) maintain that arthāpatti is an independent pramāṇa and, therefore, corresponding pramā is of a distinct kind. Their reasons for holding this view and the questions of their adequacy as also the larger question of whether or not arthāpatti is an independent pramāṇa will be considered briefly later (S 5.6). Suffice it now simply to anticipate the conclusion to be reached later and to note that it is conclusively shown by Mullatti (1977 : 119-121), that arthāpatti is reducible to inference of a very simple type and that the Naiyāyikas are right in so reducing it. If then arthāpatti is reducible to inference, the corresponding pramā reduces itself to anumiti. And as has already been shown, anumiti does satisfy the justification condition including the statement (v) (SS 2.11-15).

S 3.7. Absential pramā (anupalabdhi-pramā) :—One more kind of pramā that has been recognised by some orthodox schools. namely, Advaita-vedāntins and Bhāṭṭa-mīmāṃsakas is anupalabdhi-pramā or absential pramā. While this kind of pramā has received comparatively a scanty treatment in the traditional texts, it is this that gives rise to many interesting questions. It will be helpful to consider some of these questions before dealing directly with absential pramā. The questions that are dealt with here are : what is a fact ? What is an object ? What is the relation between fact and an object ? Are there negative facts ? What is absence (abhāva) ? What is counter positive (pratiyogi) ? What is the counter positive of the absence of an absence ?

S 3.8. What is a fact ? It is not easy to define a fact but looking to current usage of the word 'fact', one may say that a fact is contrasted with an event (Woozley 1967 : 131). It is also contrasted with an object (Wittgenstein : 1961 : 17). Both events and objects are in space and/or time but facts are neither in time nor in space nor in both (space and time). A fact is simply what is the case, or a state of affairs (Wittgenstein 1961 : 7).

Different kinds of facts have been recognised by different people, namely, atomic, negative, general and among general facts synthetic and necessary; (though even negative facts can be general and/or necessary). In his early stage Russell (1949 : 56) recognises necessary facts and so do Woozley (1967 : 133) and Hamlyn (1977 : 138). But thinkers like Quine (1960 : 247), Wittgenstein (1961 : 7) and perhaps later Russell (1951 b : 137-8) recognise only synthetic (empirical) facts. I assume here without argument that facts are synthetic and within the framework of this assumption atomic fact consists in a determinate individual having a certain property or in two or more determinate individuals being related in a certain way (Russell 1971 : 183, 1949 : 60). According to Wittgenstein (1961 : 7) an atomic fact is a combination of objects. Negative fact would be what corresponds to synthetic true negative proposition and general facts would be those which make general propositions (existential or universal) true, for example, that heat expands metals is said to be general (universal fact) and that some dogs are black is said to be general (existential) fact, that some books are not interesting is said to be a negative fact.

S 3.9. Though there are different kinds of facts recognised by different people at different times the question arises as to whether all of them are ultimate or some are ultimate and the rest are reducible to them. Following Wittgenstein (and later Russell) we may say that there are only atomic facts and that other facts are reducible to them. Though Russell in his *Philosophy of Logical*

Atomism (1971) and *our knowledge of the external world* (1949) recognises the different kinds of facts mentioned above, in his later philosophy *Human knowledge : its scope and Limits* (1951 b : 137-8) he comes round to the Tractatarian view of Wittgenstein, *i.e.*, he comes to recognise with Wittgenstein that there are only the atomic facts (Anscombe 1959 : 30) ; and that all the facts are reducible to these. Wittgenstein indeed talks of negative facts in Section 2.06, he says in that section a negative fact means non-existence of positive fact. According to him once we know all the atomic facts (*i.e.*, positive) we thereby know everything about the world and there is no need in the ultimate analysis for a knowledge of negative facts.[6] Perhaps on the basis of section 2.06 of Tractatus Anscombe (1959 : 30) and Black (1964 : 70) hold that 'negative fact' is simply the absence of an atomic fact. On this interpretation negative statement like 'Socrates is not tall' is true, not because there is a negative fact, namely, socrates is not tall but because it fails to correspond to the atomic fact that Socrates is tall. To this effect Black (1964 : 70) offers the following illustration. He considers a model universe of three objects only, namely, a, b and c. Further 'a and b' and 'b and c' are the only combinations so that there are only two facts. Since c and a are not combined it is not a fact at all. Now consider three propositions P_1, P_2 and P_3. Both P_1 and P_2 are true in virtue of their respective facts 'ab', 'bc' whereas P_3 is false. Nevertheless—P_3 is true not because of any fact which it corresponds to, but ouly because of the facts ab and bc. Thus P_1 and P_2 express the whole truth about the imagined universe and, hence, the universe consists of the facts, ab and bc only.

S 3.10. Demos (1917 : 189-95) also rejects negative facts. His reasons are partly similar to those of Wittgenstein and partly different. It is the difference between Demos and Wittgenstein that is more significant and stimulating than the similarity between the two. The similarity is that just as Wittgenstein (1961 : 13), (Anscombe 1959 : 29-30 ; Black 1964 : 70) says that by knowing all the atomic facts (positive facts), we know everything about the world, Demos also says that we do not encounter negative facts in the world. But while Wittgenstein explains negative fact as an absence of corresponding positive fact, Demos explains a negative fact by the presence of some other positive fact, which is incompatible with the corresponding positive fact. To take his own example, the negative fact that John is not at home is reduced to (or explained through) the positive fact that John is in the field. The positive fact that John is in the field is incompatible with the positive fact that John is at home which corresponds to the given fact that John is not at home. Similarly the fact that 'apple is not blue' is explained through or reduced to the fact that 'apple is red,' which fact is incompatible with the corresponding positive fact that 'apple is blue'. This position of Demos is very significantly different from that of Wittgenstein. For Wittgenstein the supposed negative fact that apple is not blue is simply the absence of the positive fact that 'apple is blue'.

S 3.11. Curiously enough Russell in his early phase (1914), especially in 1918 recognises negative facts even though he is fully aware of Demos's rejection of them. In fact he explicitly repudiates Demos. Russell's (1971 : 211-16) arguments for the negative facts are :

(i) A negative statement like Socrates is not alive cannot be made true unless there are corresponding negative facts. This by itself seems to beg the question but amongst the examples that Russell gives there is one which is apparently plausible, namely, the true negative statement, "There is no hippopotamus in this room." On Demos's view this statement has got to be made true by the presence of some other positive fact. But what is the positive fact which plays this role ? That fact, as Russell (1971 : 213) insists, "cannot be merely that every part of this room is filled up with something that is not a hippopotamus." Perhaps a more plausible example would seem to be a true negative statement "Unicorns do not exist" (or "There are no unicorns"). Surely there cannot be any single positive fact (or even a series of them) in the world which would validate this later statement. The difference between the former example and the latter may be said to be that the former refers to relative non-existence and the later to absolute non-existence. However, these examples are only apparently plausible. They really miss the point as I show a little later on.

(ii) Demos's contention that a true negative statement is made true by some other positive fact which is inconsistant with the corresponding positive fact, is untenable according to Russell. Russell holds that the incompatibility between the two facts is itself a negative fact. Russell (1971 : 213-4) is able to advance this argument because at this phase of his thought he recognises general facts of logic and inconsistency is surely a fact of logic. But if facts are restricted to empirical facts as I have stipulated (S 3.8) then it is hard to see how inconsistency between facts or propositions could itself be a negative fact.

(iii) Russell's third argument for negative fact is that since no one can object to the recognition of absence of positive facts, there should be no objection to the recognition of negative facts also. This argument is odd, to say the least, for, from the primary existence of negative fact, it eliminates the whole case for negative facts. For as seen above Wittgenstein and his followers deny the ultimacy to negative facts on the ground that they reduce to absence of positive facts. Further, this argument hardly makes sense in the context of Demos's position as just noted above for Demos a negative fact is explained by the presence of some other positive fact and not by the absence of a positive fact. It is to Demos's position that Russell is immediately reacting.

S 3.12. I have briefly pointed out the deficiency in Russell's second and third arguments for negative facts. Let me now return to his first argument. Russell's example "There is no hippopotamus in this room" and the other example suggested by me, "There are no unicorns", are not really denials of atomic facts. They are negative existentials and the status of existentials whether negative or positive is beyond the scope of my present discussion. Even so it may be pointed out that Russell himself recognises general facts and the two negative existentials are indeed general facts. As such they demand a separate analysis. These examples are beside the point and do not disprove Demos. For they are general (not simple) in character while Demos confines his attention to simple negative facts, *i.e.*, denials of atomic facts. They cannot, in other words, prove the existence of (simple) negative facts. Nor in fact do they prove the existence of general facts. For even though Russell in his early phases recognised general facts, he came to realise in his later phase that general facts whether positive or negative, are ultimately explained in terms of atomic facts.

S 3.13 Thus none of Russell's arguments for negative facts is adequate and, therefore, Russell's acceptance of them in his early phase is not warranted. Russell himself came to realise this subsequently and in his *Human knowledge* : *its scope and limits* (1951b : 137-42) gives up negative facts. His arguments for doing so are just those of Demos *i.e.*, the alleged negative fact is explained as the presence of some 'atomic fact'. To take Russell's own examples :

(i) "This is not salt" is explained in terms of positive fact (atomic fact), "This is sugar." Similarly,

(ii) "This butter cap is not red" is reduced to "This butter cup is yellow."

Russell does not explicitly consider the one example which appeared to him earlier to support the thesis of negative facts, namely, "There is no hippopotamus in this room." As I have pointed out earlier this is a negative existential and Russell used it earlier because he then accepted general facts whether positive or negative, but in his *Human Knowledge* : *its scope and limits* (1951b : 149-51) along with negative facts he rejects general facts also so that the possibility of a general negative fact is ruled out. A universal fact was explained as a conjunction of a series of atomic facts and an existential fact was reduced to a disjunction of series of atomic facts. Thus a negative general fact *i.e.*, either a negative universal fact or negative existential fact was reduced either to negation of a conjunction or to a negation of disjunction. And thus the latter are ultimately reduced by Russell to the presence of some atomic fact or the other.

S 3.14 Thus the difference between Demos and Wittgenstein noted above reappears as the difference between the Russell and Wittgenstein with regard to the status of negative facts. In other words while Wittgenstein (1961 : 13) treates a negative fact as ultimately the *absence* of some atomic (fact(s), Russell (1951b : 138) treats it as the *presence* of some atomic fact(s). It is interesting to note that this difference between the two thinkers does not interfere with their logic, for both of them a negative statement is a truth functional statement and the rule of negation, namely, that the negation of a true statement is false and that the negation of false statement is true. But in so far as a negative fact is taken to be what corresponds to a true negative statement it is difficult to see how a difference in the conception of the nature of a negative fact cannot have repurcusions, on the repurcusions on the views of two thinkers regarding the nature of the negative statements. In other words, one would expect that a difference in the accounts by the two thinkers of the nature of negative facts would be reflected in their accounts of the nature of negative statements. That this is not so seem to show that one of the two accounts regarding the nature of negative facts is wrong. I cannot argue this point here but I believe that it is Russell's account that is wrong. Henceforward therefore, I accept Wittgenstein's view that a negative fact is, in the ultimate analysis, is simply, the absence of the corresponding atomic fact (s). A negative fact may be simple, truth functional or general. The examples of these three kinds of facts are respectively expressed by the sentences :

$\sim$Fa, $\sim$ ($\exists$x)(Fx) or $\sim$ (Fa & Ga) or $\sim$ (Fa v Ga), $\sim$(x) (Fx) The fact expressed by '$\sim$Fa' is reduced to the absence of the fact expressed by 'Fa', the fact expressed by $\sim$ (Fa & Ga) is reduced to the one or the other of the three facts, namely, "$\sim$ Fa & $\sim$ Ga", $\sim$ Fa & Ga and "Fa & $\sim$ Ga." These conjunctions themselves are ultimately reduced to atomic facts or their absences. For the fact expressed by the conjunction 'Fa&Ga' is reduced to the two atomic facts, Fa' and 'Ga' and the same principle is applied in the conjunction of more complicated types. Similarly the fact expressed by 'Fa v Ga' is reduced to either 'Fa' or 'Ga' or both and the same principle is a applied to disjunction of a more involved character. General facts are reduced ultimately to either conjunction or disjunction of elementary facts.

S 3.15 Thus while the fact that one may talk of negative facts does not by itself show that a negative fact is accorded an independent logical status. As has just been shown a negative fact is *ultimately* reducible to absence of an atomic fact. Inspite of its reducibility one may choose to talk about a negative fact because of practical convenience as distinct from theoretical necessity. Now to say that a negative fact is ultimately reduciable to the absence of some atomic fact is to say it is an absence. But there are different kinds of absences and at this juncture it is important to distinguish between the absence of fact and the absence of a thing or object. A fact as Wittgenstain (S 3.8) has said is a combination of objects and as object or a thing can be though it need not be a constituent of a fact. While the absence of a fact corresponds to a true negative statement (just an as atomic fact corresponds to a true atomic sentence) the absence of a thing or an object corresponds to a non-empty negative term. In the case of a negative term, question of truth value does not arise but only the question of applicability or reference. A negative term and a negative sentence are two different syntactic categories and are generated in different ways. The standard way of generating the negation of a sentence is to prefix the negation operator "∼" to that sentence. There is no standard way of generating a negative term but one may devise a term operator such as "—" and prefix it to a (positive) term. But there can be no doubt that a negative fact cannot be reduced to the absence of a thing. On a linguistic plane this has the consequence that a negative statement cannot be reduced to a negative term (in English). A term is not a statement, it can only be a constituent of a statement.

S 3.16 This important distinction between the absence of a fact and the absence of a thing and negative statement and negative term and hence between a statement and term is not clearly maintained in the Indian tradition. Ingalls (1951 : 55) says:

> The Naiyāyika does not make a distinction between negating a term and negating a statement of formula. To him all absences are single terms, for they can all be expressed by a single compound word.

For example, "Fire is a locus of mutual absence of water" (vahnirjalanyonyābhāvavān). This is indeed true because of the peculiarity of Sanskrit language. But this does not affect the fact, the underlying thought that the absence of fact cannot be reduced to the absence of a thing, whatever be the linguistic media.[7]

S 3.17 A textual definition of absence as given in SM 12 is: abhāvatvaṃ dravyādiṣaṭkānyonyābhāvatvam. "Non-existance is that which is possessed of the mutual non-existence (*i.e.*, difference) in respect of the six categoties beginning with substance." (Translated by Madhavananda 1977 : 16).

This definition obviously begs the question as Athalye (1974 : 101 rightly points out. It uses the conception of special variety of absence in defining the concept of absence in general. Another definition which seems to be more plausible but in fact is not is the one given by Annaṃbhaṭṭa, namely, 'absence is opposed to the existence of the counterpositive'.[8] Annaṃbhaṭṭa's definition is based on Gaṅgeśa's definition of absence. Matilal (1968 ; 94) says:

> An absence, as a property, is necessarily dependent upon a counterpositive. This feature of dependence upon a counterpositive is urged by Gaṅgeśa as the necessary character of an absence.

Again Matilal (1968 : 56) says:

> It is obvious that to define even the notion of absence-ness or hostility we must use the notion of counterpositiveness in turn.

Annaṃbhaṭṭa's definition avoids an explicit petitio but it is guilty of circularity. Abhāva is defined in terms of concept of counterpositive or pratiyogi. But the rerm pratiyogi itself connot be defined without the concept of absence (abhāva). As Matilal (1968 : 59) says:

> Whatever the status of counterpositiveness, one thing is clear: this abstract concept is entirely dependent upon the concept of absence.

One popular definition of pratiyogi is 'yasyābhāvaḥ sa pratiyogī' *i.e.*, "Counterpositive is that whose absence (*is spoken of*)", (cited in Matilal 1968a : 52, fn 2). This definition obviously makes use of the notion of absence (abhāva).[9]

S 3.18 This circularity of conceiving abhāva in terms of pratiyogi and conceiving pratiyogi in terms of abhāva is sought to be avoided by the Prābhākara school of Pūrva-mīmāṃsā. This school identifies the absence of a thing with the locus of that absence.[10] To take an example, the absence of a pot is the same as the ground in which the absence is said to reside. In this definition of absence, the recources to the notion of counterpositive is entirely avoided because the notion of absence itself is eliminated in favour of someting positive. But of course the Prābhākaras do not succeed in such an elimination because locus is itself a relative term and cannot be fully understood without reference to that which resides in it. As soon as the ground is described as a locus, the question arises, "locus of what" and the question can only be answered by saying "locus of the absence of pot." So as soon as we try to understand what the locus in question is the notion of locus creeps in and the Prābhākara's attempt to define it away crumbles. Gaṅgeśa rejects the Prabhākara's identification of absence with locus but on very dubious grounds. He says that absence of a pot cannot be reduced to the ground in which it resides because it is something over and above the ground that this is so follows according to him by the fact that the ground with pot and ground without pot are two different entities (Vidyabhusana 1971 : 415-6). This is a dubious consideration because it is not at all clear how the difference between the ground with pot and ground without pot entails the independence and externality of the absence of pot. In any case Gaṅgeśa insists that the concept of abhāva cannot be understood without reference to the concept of the counterpositive, and thereby lays himself open to the above objection.

S 3.19 Traditionally absences have been distinguished namely, prior absence (prāgabhāva), posterior absence (dhvamsābhāva), absolute or constant absence (atyantābhāva) and mutual absence (anyonyābhāva).[11] The prior absence of a thing is absence of that thing before it comes into being. It is said to be beginningless but to (have) an end. It comes to an end when the thing in question comes into being. But prior to the coming into being in question the absence of that being stretches endlessly. This assumes of course that an object has continuous existence in time and/or place. However, such an assumption is not universally accepted in Indian tradition itself, especially in mythological contexts, for instance, both surās and asurās are said to have power of coming into being and passing out of being at will. They are thus said to be discontinuous or jerky existences. Therefore, in this case prior absence cannot be said to be endless. A similar consideration also applies to posterior absence. This is the absence of a given thing after it ceases to be. This absence is said to have beginning but no end. But the case just referred to disproves this claim. Posterior absence is no more unending than prior absence is beginningless. These two varieties of absence are really unimportant. It is the remaining two varieties that deserve a close scrutiny. Absolute absence is defined as absolutely eternal *i.e.*, it holds at all times past, present and future unlike prior and posterior absence which have either a beginning or an end but eternal otherwise *i.e.*, their eternality is one-sided. An obsolute absence is also said to be a denial of relation other than identity (Ingalls 1951 : 54-5). Such a relation may be of different kinds, namely, contract (saṃyoga), inherence (samavāya), qualifier-ness (viśeṣaṇatā or svarūpa). It excludes of course identity (tādātmya) which is also a relation. Examples of such an absence are :

(i) The absence of a jar on the ground,

(ii) The absence of colour in the air,

and (iii) The absence of fire in the lake.

S 3.20 The problem that immediately springs to one's mind is as to why absolute absence is described as eternal. Surely the absence of a pot on the ground is not eternal but limited to a certain duration of time, since the pot in question at different duration of time could be placed on the ground in question. The traditional answer to this question is rather strange, namely, that the absence of the jar on the ground is the denial of samavāya sambandha or inherent relation and that this denial holds even when the pot is present on the ground because the pot can only be present by saṃayoga sambandha (the relation of contract) not by the relation of inherence. The nature of atyantābhāva can be made clearer in contract with the next variety of absence, namely, anyonyābhāva (mutual absence). This type of abhāva is said to be the denial of identity relation (unlike atyantābhāva which is the dential of a relation other than identity). An example of anyonyābhāva is that the pat is not cloth (ghaṭaḥ pato na). The same example is also sometimes expressee in what Matilal (1968a : 16,28) calls property location, when thus it is expressed, the example will take the form: 'ghaṭe phatābhavaḥ' or 'paṭe ghaṭāhāva ca'. There is a controversy regarding whether anyonyābhāva is also eternal. The Naiyāyikas hold that it is eternal (Bhattacarya 1975;68), their argument is that the difference between any two things recognised to be distinct does not begin or end in time, and hence is eternal. But this view of course is wrong for more than one reasons. Firstly, it commits us to essentialism that is the view that there are rigidly characterised and fixed species in the world and that there is no question of their intermingling or inter-action and that these species are eternally given, but this is a doctrine which has long been shown to be untenable (Armstrong 1978-61-7). Secondly, it also commits us to the view that a true denial of an identity or more precisely a true negation of an identity is itself a logical or eternal truth. And a false identity statement would be self contradiction. But as the modern theory of identity has shown this is just not true. There are identity statements which are contingently false and there are other identity statements which are contingently true and the negation of such identities would also be contingent. Examples are :

(i) Mount Everest is Gauriśaṅkara; is contingently true identity statement and so is

(ii) Mount Everest is the highest mountain in the world.
An example of contingently false identity statement is Marktwain is John Swift.

This of course does not mean that all identity statements are contingent, there are also true identity statements which are logically true. There are also identity statements which are logically false. For example; 'Plato is Plato' is logically true identity statement and 'Plato is not Plato' is logically false identity statement.

The Advaitins seem to have glimpsed the substance of these criticisms because they argue that anyonyābhāva is not necessarily eternal; it may be eternal in some cases while non-eternal in some other cases, it all depends according to them, on the nature of the things, the identity between which is truly denied (Datta 1972:181). If the things are in time then a true denial of identity is contingent *i.e.*, non-eternal while if the things in question are eternal then a true denial is necessarily true or eternal.

S 3.21 The examples of atyantābhāva and anyonyābhāva are likely to mislead one into thinking that they are really one and the same. For example, when it is said that 'fire is the locus of the mutual absence of water' and that 'the lake is the locus of the constant adsence of fire (Ingalis 1951:54-5), one is tempted to say in the latter case also that lake is different from fire just as in the former case. One natuarally says that fire is different from water, one must guard against this temptation because the two kinds of absences are really different. The kinds of relation denied in two cases are different. Atyantābhāva in a sense implies anyonyābhāva thought not conversely. It says something more than anyonyābhāva. When it is said that 'there is absence of the pot on the ground' then it is implied that ground and the pot are different (the same implication is of couse carried also by the statement that there is the presence of the pot on the ground). But atyantābhāva is said to say something further, namely, that none of the relations: contact (saṃyoga), inherence (samavāya) and qualifierness (svarūpa) holds (Athalye 1974:366). But this position creates a problem. If absolute absence (atyantābhāva) is denial or relation other than identity then surely it cannot carry the implication of the denial of identity for there cannot be anything in the conclusion of a deductive inference that is not already there in its premisses. But if the denial of identity is already there in atyantābhāva then atyantābhāva cannot be merely the denial of relation other than identity, it has also got to be the denial of the relation including identity. The solution to this problem seems to be that the reflexivity of identity is a universal phenomenon and, therefore, a true denial of reflexivity has also got to be a universal phenomenon and as such it is implied in any true denial of a relation other than identity. Ingalls (1951:55) says :

> . . . (atyantābhāva), the absence of a thing somewhere, when this absence is not limited to a portion of time.

It is difficult to see how the absence of the pot on the ground satisfies the requirement as thus formulated by Ingalls, for while the absence of the pot is somewhere, namely, on the ground it is still limited by time as the Advaitins are quick to point out. Yet the absence of the pot on the ground is said to be a case of atyantābhāva if it is replied that what is meant is the absence of inherence (the samavāya, a relation other than identity) in the case of the absence of the jar. But the absence of inherence (samavāyaḥ) is also there even in the presence of the pot on the ground. So there is a sense in which we can talk about any presence (not merely a special case of absence) as a case of atyantābhāva. But this is indeed an odd consequence and I confess that I do not know how to handle it.

S 3.22 It has been remarked above that concept of absence cannot be understood without reference to the concept of counterpositive. This means any difference in counterpositive results in a different absence. For example the absence of the pot is different from the absence of cloth because counterpositives of two absences are different. This does not mean however, that a difference in absence necessarily means difference in counterpositive. In other words, absence may be different and yet their counterpositive may be the same. For example, with reference to the same pot you can have prior absence (prāgabhāva), and posterior absence (dhvamasābhāva) as also absolute absence (atyantābhāva) and mutual absence (anyonyābhava). And also trivialty there cannot be more than one counterpositive for a given absence.

S 3.23 An important question that is discussed in Nyāya is whether the absence of the absence of a thing is the same as that thing. Or symbolically whether

(i) — — a = a (Ingalls 1951:68)

(The sign '—' is used to symbolise any kind of absence. And the sign '=' is meant for identity (tādātmya)). Gaṅgeśa and Mathurānāth accept (i) (Ingalls 1951:68; Athalye 1974:368)[12] but Raghunātha (and Gadadhara) (Matilal 1968a:57) reject it (Ingalls 1951: 68; Athalye 1974:368). Raghunātha's argument is :

> The point is that all absences have as their nature absence (abhavatva), an imposed property according to Raghunātha, the nature of the seventh category according to the conservatives, and no amount of legerdemain can turn these absence into entitles whose nature is presence (bhāvatva), a different imposed property according to Raghunātha, the nature of the first six categories according to the conservatives. (Ingalls 1951:68).

But while rejecting (i) Raghunātha accepts

(ii) — — — a = — a

But in doing so Raghunātha seems to be inconsistent, as can be easily shown. From (ii) it follows :

(iii) — — — a ≠ — a

Because if the counterpositives (c) are different their corresponding absences would be different (S 3.22). And the counterpositives here are different :

C of — — — a = a and C of — a is a

But — — a ≠ a according to Raghunātha, (iii) is the very denial of (i). Again arguing from (i) we can say :

(iv) C of — — — a = C of — a

Identical absences have identical counterpositives.

entities denied by essentially identical entities are themselves essentially identical. (Ingalls 1951:71) *i.e.*,

(v) ——a=a

(v) is the very denial of (ii). So Raghunātha is inconsistent, in accepting (ii) and rejecting (i), even within the Nyāya system, they are of course inconsistent also by independent logical considerations. Of these two inconsistent statements it is obviously (i) that needs to be rejected, since (ii) is universsally accepted (including the opponent Mathurānātha on the one hand and Raghunātha on the other). (ii) obviously follows from (i) but (i) does not follow from (ii) though the analogy of our standard predicate logic, seems to suggest that (i) does indeed follow from (ii) (the use of the word analogy is deliberate here '—a,' — —a' and '— — —a' being expression of absences as against negations, are not well formed formulas in our standard predicate logic).

S 3.24. A related question is whether or not one can talk about the counterpositive of absence of an absence. On Gaṅgeśa's (and Mathurānātha's) (S 3.23) view we really cannot for (i) shows that absence of an absence ceases to be an absence and converts itself into presence and it makes no sense to talk about the counterpositive of presence (S 3.23). However, according to Raghunātha absence of absence of 'a' is still an absence and therefore, is quite distinct from a presence. It does, therefore, have a counterpositive and the counterpositive can only be the absence of 'a'. [A noteworthy fact that emerges from this consideration, is that a counterpositive can itself be an absence and this is quite consistent with the characterisation of a counterpositive given above (S 3.d7)].

It is this consequence that was used in showing up of the inconsistency of Raghunātha.

S 3.25. Having discussed the preliminary but interesting questions that arise with regard to absential pramā (anupalabdhi pramā), I now proceed to a direct account of this kind of pramā. The clearest definition of 'anupalabdhi pramā' is to be found in 'Vedānta-paribhāṣa's definition of anupalabdhi-pramāṇa which is :

abhāvānubhavāsādhāraṇakāraṇamanupalabdhi rūpaṃ pramāṇam. "The instrumental cause of true cognition of absence is called anupalabdhi pramāṇa." VP 125.

This definition clearly shows that anupalabdhi pramā is true cognition of absence. The absence is usually meant for the absence of an entity rather than of a fact. On the face of it, it seems rather strange that the Advaitins should recognise an independent pramāṇa for (true) cognition of an absence. But closer examination shows that their position is not entirely baseless. The only and the most obvious alternative according an independent status to anupalabdhi pramāṇa would be, for the Advaitins to reduce it to perception for even the possibility of reducing anupalabdhi pramāṇa to any of the other pramāṇas does not exist. But the Vedāntins do not take this only available possibility because by its very definition, perception consists in sense object contact (indriyāratha sannikarṣa) and there cannot be any sense object contact in the case of anupalabdhi pramā. For the Naiyāyikas absence is a category and therefore, for them sense-object contact is maintained even in the case of anupalabdhi pramā, and anupalabdhi pramā becomes simply a case of perception. But what is baffling is the position of the Bhāṭṭās in this regard, they too like the Naiyāyikas recognise absence as a category.[13] This would mean that even for them sense-object contact would be maintained in the case of anupalabdhi pramā which, therefore, would be simply a case of perceptual pramā. In other words the Bhāṭṭās' recognition of categorial status of absence commits them to reducing anupalabdhi pramā to perception, just as the Naiyāyikas do. Yet oddly enough the Bhāṭṭās regard anupalabdhi as an independent pramāṇa. The Naiyāyikas counter this position of the Advaitins by saying that an absence can be perceived by the same sense-organ which perceives its counterpositive. But this account would by itself be ineffective against the Vadāntins because they would reply back by saying that if absence could indeed be perceived it would falsify the generally accepted definition of percebtion in terms of sense-object contact. If this drastic consequence is to be avoided, they would insist that absence cannot be apprehended by perception but needs an independent pramāṇa. What makes the Naiyāyikas' position defective is their assumption, though not explicitly brought into play in this context, that absence is a category. The categorial status of absence brings it on the same level as substance (dṛvya) and makes it possible a sense-object contact even in the case of absence. Since Advaitins do not recognise absence as a category they have no way of manipulating sense-object contact in the case of absence. They are constrained to recognise an independent pramāṇa for absential pramā. But this makes the Bhāṭṭās' position quite baffling for they recognise not only anupalabdhi as an independent pramāṇa but also absence as an independent category. (MN 133-45 ; 289-310). As it should be clear from the foregoing paragraph, either of these two assumptions makes the other superfluous, if anupalabdhi is accorded an independent status. There is no need to recognise absence as a separate category to account for absential pramā. If on the other hand apsence is regarded as a category, there is no need to accord an independent status to anupalabdhi pramāṇa. But to say that either of these assumptions makes the other superfluous is not to say that the two are logically incompatible. In other words the Bhāṭṭās'acceptance of both the assumptions is not a logical flaw but stylistic one to suffer from the fallacy of heaviness (gaurava).

S 3.26. As in the case of perception so in the caee of anupalabdhi the same word is used for both the pramāṇa and pramā in question. While in the case of perception there is not much difficulty in maintaining the distinction between pramā and pramāṇa ; in the case of anupalabdhi it is not easy to maintain the distinction as to what is anupalabdhi pramā. The Vedānta-paribhāṣā definition quoted above makes it clear that it is a (true) cognition of absence, but what is the pramāṇa of such a true cognition ? Sometimes it is absence that is said to be the instrumental cause (MN ; 133 Matilal 1968 a : 99-100). Clearly such an answer will not do. Absence is what is known as prameya (knowable object) surely and cannot be a pramāṇa. If anupalabdhi is reduced to perception then of course the pramā, pramāṇa distinction could equally be maintained. But the difficulty arises as soon as it is accorded an independent status.

The difficulties regarding the status of anupalabdhi stem from the metaphysical beliefs of the contending schools and partly from the traditional definition of perception consisting in sense-object contact. As today's psychology of perception has clearly shown such a definition is misleading to say the least. Perception does need contact even in an extended sense and the absence of an object can be apprehended by perception as thc presence of that object. The metaphysical beliefs regarding the categorial status of absence have played this role in observing the simple fact. The Bhāṭṭās and Advaitins were simply wrong in giving an independent status to anupalabdhi as a pramāṇa and anupalabdhi pramā simply it is a case of pratyakṣa pramā ; as such it satisfies the condition (v) of knowledge as pointed out, the justifying statement(s) must be known to be true (S 2.10).

S 3.27. It thus seems that all the different forms of pramā satisfy the condition (v) of knowledge (SS 1.4-5). It has already been noticed that they satisfy truth condition and belief condition (SS 2.3-8) and the satisfaction of the condition (v) means the satisfaction of the justification condition. I, therefore, conclude that pramā, since it satisfies all conditions of knowledge, is the traditional Indian counterpart of the contemporary western concept of knowledge. I shall, therefore, hence forward translate pramā as knowledge.

S 3.28. The foregoing discussion of the nature of pramā is likely to invite the charge of circularity. For I have defined it as 'pramā karṇaṃ pramāṇam' (fn 0.3) ; in other words I have relied on the notion of pramā in defining pramāṇa ; eventually however in analysing the concept of pramā especially in distinguishing the different kinds of pramā, I have in turn depended on the notion of pramāṇa. For example, I have said that anumiti is that which is produced by anumāna, *i.e.*, inferential pramāṇa (S 2.11) that upamiti, *i.e.*, identificational pramā is that which is produced by upamāna, *i.e.*, identificational pramāṇa (S 3.3) and so on. There is thus mutual dependence (anyonyāśrya) of pramā and pramāṇa in my discussion. One may plausibly interpret this mutual dependence as circularity in reasoning and a conceptual flaw.

In attenuation of the circularity in my treatment of the nature of pramā, I can only plead as Wiggins (1965 : 68-70) does ; that when the mutual definition of two concepts is unavoidable in a given context the concepts in question are basic or primitive. When one is dealing with the very fundamental concepts, reference to one another in the process of their clarification is hardly avoidable and it would be pedantic to regard such mutual dependence as a flaw.

Of course within a formal or artificial language a primitive term is strictly an undefined term, and there is no question of interdepending of the primitives of a given artificial language. But this sense of premitiveness is relative to a given formal system what is premitive in one system need not be such [in another system, and there is no special sanctity or significance to the primitives of a system apart from their purely functional aspects. But in the discussion of the nature of pramā we are not dealing with the elements of an artificial language where symbols have predetermined and absolutely precise significance but with the natural and living language. In other words we are up against epistemological primitives as against logical ones, and in the case of the basic or primitive concepts of a natural language there is no relativity, their fundamental coherence is absolute not geared to the nature of specific theory or system. And this goes for epistemological primitives also ; these are fundamental concepts underlying our thought and discourse in general, and their fundamental character is absolute, Hence in clarifying any such concepts a reference to some similar concept or concepts is inevitable and such mutual reference can by no means count as a defect.[14]

Notes and References

1. kaścidgavayaśabdārthamajānankutaścidāraṇyakapuruṣādgosadṛśo gavaya iti śrutvā vanaṃ gato vākyātrthaṃ smarangosadṛśam piṇḍaṃ piṇḍaṃ paśyati tadanantaramasā gavaya śabdavācya ityupamitirutpadyate. A person, not knowing the meaning of the word gavaya, and hearing from a certain forester, (the sentence) 'A gavaya is similar to a cow,' and then going to the forest, sees a (live) body similar to (that of) of a cow, while remembering the meaning of that sentence. After this, there arises (in that person) the knowledge from analogy, 'That is what is denoted by the word "agavya". TS 58. Translated by C. Bhattacharya 1975:153. SM 80.
2. SM 81; TD 59; Athalye 1974:333: Mullatti 1977:27.
3. nagareṣu dṛṣṭgopiṇdasya puruṣasya vanaṃ gatasya gavayenidriyasannikarṣe sati bhavati pratītiḥ, 'ayaṃ piṇdo gosadṛśaḥ' iti. tandanantaranca bhavati niscayaḥ. 'anena sadṛśī madīyā gauḥ' iti. "A man who has seen a cow's from in cities and has gone to a forest, where his eyes have come in contact with a gyal (gavaya), has the cognition, 'this thing like a cow.' Then he has the conviction, 'my cow is like this.' VP 83. Translated by Madhavananda 1972:83. Chatterjee 1939:327-8; Datta 1972:145; Satprakasananda 1974:153-4.

4. āptavākyaṃ śabdaḥ. "The verbal instrument of knowledge is a sentence of a trustworthy person." TS 59. Translated by Bhattacharya 1975:158, NS 1.1.7. vākyārthajñānaṃ śābdajñānam. tat karaṇaṃ śabdaḥ. "Verbal cognition is the knowledge of the meaning of a sentence. The instrument of this (verbal knowledge) is words." "TS 63" Translated by Bhattacharya 1975:195. VP 86,112-5.

5. yathā rātribhojanena vinā divāabhunjānasya pīnatvamanupapannam. "As, the stoutness of a man who does not eat at day time is inexplicable unless we assume his eating at night." "VP 117. Translated by Madhavananda 1972:117.

6. ' The world is the totality of facts, not of things,' Wittgenstein 1961:7. "The totality of existing states of affairs also determines which states of affairs do not exist." Wittgenstein 1961:13.

"The totality of facts determines what is the case and whatever is not the case." Wittgenstein 1961:7.

7. Ingalls equates absences with the denials of relations including identity. But his treatment is suspect for variety of reasons not pursued here.

8. abhāvānnāstīti tarkitapratigogissatvavirodhi. . . TD 43.

9. The concept of counterpositive has been discussed in detail in *TCDG* Tattva—Cintāmaṇi-dīdhiti-gādhādhari 357-8. The discussion begins with a tentative definition which is progressively modified as and when it is found to be defective. (Matilal (1968:59-6) mentions four such modifications, D^1 to D^4 and each one of these including D^4 which is the final modification is rejected as unsatisfactory. The upshot of the whole discussion is that the concept of counterpositive cannot be defined without reference to the concept of absence (abhāva) *i.e.*, without involving circularity.

10. atha kevalamadhikaraṇaṃ tajajñānaṃ vā abhāvaḥ sa cāpratiyogikaeva. "Now. . .that the mere locus or a cognition thereof is (*all that*) absence (amounts to) that this occurs without any counterpositive." (Cited in Matilal 1961a:181, 129).

11. abhāvaścaturvidhaḥ. prāgabhāvaḥ pradhvaṃsābhāvoatyantābhāvoanyonyābhāvasceti TS 9. BP 12; VP 137.

12. Athalye (1974:368) uses the word ancient for conservatives of Navyanaiyāyikas which is rather misleading. Ingails improves upon Athalye by using the word conservative.

13. . . .abhāvākhyaṃ padārthaṃ ca pañcamaṃ cintayāmahe. ". . .we consider the fifth category, too, called non-existence." MN 289. Translated by Raja and Śastri 1975:289 Hiriyanna 1973:324; Radhakrishnan 1977b:416.

14. It might be suggested in reply to this charge that although the definition of pramāṇa involves a reference to the concept of pramā, the definition of pramā stated does not involve a reference to pramāṇa. In fact an independent definition of pramā has been given in the Indian tradition, namely pramā, is that which corresponds to reality (tadvati tatprakārko anubhavo yathārthah. . . sa eva pramā . . . TS 35). This is indeed so in general. Nevertheless the manner in which I have developed the discussion is open to charge of circularity as explained above.

4

WHAT IS PRAMĀṆA ?

S 4.1. In view of the conclusion reached above, namely, that pramā essentially answers to the contemporary concept of knowledge, it may not be wrong to hold that a pramāṇa is a source of *knowledge*. Such a view is familiar enough and readily agrees with our common sense and ordinary practice. Even in ordinary life we often classify what we consider to be cases of knowledge as perceptual, inferential, testimonial etc. The so-called sources of knowledge may be certain faculties of our mind (*e.g.*, perception, inference, memory etc.). There is reason to believe that traditionally even such sources as testimony (śabda), identification (upamāna), postulation (arthāpatti) etc. are regarded as faculties. Or at least a plausible case could be made that they are so regarded. In so regarding the pramāṇas, the traditional thinkers often mixed up psychological questions on the one hand and epistemologicat and logical ones on the other. My interest naturally is to isolate, as far as possible, the epistemological issues and try, within my limitation, to deal with them with regard to śabdā (testimony), which is the main concern of this thesis.

S 4.2. An epistemological question that needs to be raised in this conection is whether the so-called pramāṇas of traditional Indian thought are sources of knowledge only or sources of false beliefs also. The definition of pramāṇa that was considered at length earlier (fn 0.3), that pramāṇa is a source or instrumental cause of knowledge seems on the face of it to allow the possibility of pramāṇa being the source of false belief as well. And this goes for some other expressions habitually employed in connection with pramāṇas, namely, "valid sources of knowledge," "sources of valid knowledge," and "valid source of true cognition." Really speaking these different expressions are not synonymous. For example, "valid source of knowledge" and "source of valid knowledge" do not have the same meaning. In the former expression the epithet "valid" qualifies pramāṇa thereby suggesting the theoretical possibility of an invalid source of knowledge (pramāṇa). In the latter expression, on the other hand, the same epithet qualifies knowledge but does so vacuously ; for "valid" in this context means 'true' or 'adequate', and hence "true knowledge" carries no more information, than just "knowledge." As seen before, knowledge by definition is true (S 1.3). However, despite their subtle difference in meaning, these expressions are treated in actual practice as synonymous by traditional thinkers ; and they continue to be treated by secondary authors even today.

S 4.3. It is not as if the epistemological question just referred to is being raised only in modern times : it was raised in the tradition itself and answered explicitly by saying that a pramāṇa is a source of knowledge only. It is also possible to argue that an opposite answer is present at least implicitly in the tradition. It is, therefore, desirable to survey the traditional arguments, explicit or implicit, for and against the view that pramāṇas are exclusively sources of knowledge.

Explicit textual evidence is all along in favour of the view that pramāṇas are sources of knowledge only. An early author like Vātsyāyana (400 A.D.) says that instruments of knowledge *always* apprehend things as they are.[1] This clearly means that pramāṇās cannot be the sources of anything but knowledge. Śaṅkara (788 A.D.—820 A.D.) makes the same point almost in the same words.[2] Śivāditya (1100 A.D.) is even more explicit and says that pramāṇa is that which is always in invariable connection with pramā, *i.e.*, knowledge.[3] Jayanta-bhaṭṭa (965 A.D.) is equally emphatic in observing that pramāṇa is the cause which produces non-erroneous cognition of objects.[4] Viśvanātha (1700 A.D.) echoes the same view and he says that the (instrumental) cause of knowledge is different from the cause of false beliefs.[5] There are of course statements which, taken in isolation and out of context, seem to suggest that pramāṇas could also be the sources of apramā or false belief, for example, Vātsyāyana himself says pramāna is a source of cognition.' Similarly Viśvanātha associates the four types of cognition (as against true cognition) with the four pramāṇas.[7] But such statements are not to be taken in their proper context : they mean that the pramāṇas are exclusively sources of knowledge and their authors have themselves confirmed this point.[8]

S 4.4. All available explicit evidence is in favour of the view that pramāṇa is source of knowledge only. However, common sense is strongly against this view and resistance to it is reflected in the views of at least some notable secondary authors. For example, Athalye (1974 : 211) clearly says that the pramāṇās are to be taken as sources of both pramā and apramā. And D.M. Datta (1972 : 347) argues along the same line. But so long as textual evidence does not support their view, these authors cannot be taken seriously. After all even on the face of common sense traditional thinkers (in fact any thinker) are free to use their terms in the way they like so long as they define them adequately. The real criticism of the textually supported view comes, therefore, not from such secondary authors but from internal tensions within the tradition itself. Such tensions may be regarded as providing implicit or, indirect evidence for the opposite view, namely, the pramāṇas are also sources of false belief.

S 4.5. The view that pramāṇas are the sources of knowledge only means in effect that the pramāṇa employed in arriving at a cognition is itself a sufficient condition and a guarantee for the truth of that cognition. For instance, if the cognition that the city square is on fire, is said to come from a perception that is by itself a proof conclusive of the cognition's truth. No further investigation is needed, in other words, no empirical proposition especially aiomic ones would ever be false nor would they be even may be called in question. It is a common place that the statements based on sense-experience are continuously called in question and revised. And this seems to be indeed admitted by the Indian thinkers themselves inspite of their definition of pramāṇa referred to above (fn 0.3), for instance a commonly accepted definition of truth in the Indian tradition is the one noticed earlier (fn 1.2) that 'a true cognition is what corresponds to reality' *i.e.*, truth of cognition is to be determined by means of the considerations outside itself, consideration pertaining to reality. This is also emphasised by 'the doctrine of the extrinsic validity of knowledge' (parataḥ-prāmāṇya-vāda). Pointing in the same direction is the traditional view that a vyāpti (pervasion) is known to be true on the basis of frequent observation (bhūvodarśanena. TS 45 ; VP 72).

S 4.6. It may be thought that just as the tradittonal definition of truth, parataḥ-prāmāṇya-vāda, and the traditional view regarding the establishment of vyāpti provide indirect or implicit evidence for the view that pramāṇas are not exclusively the sources of knowledge, so also the traditional theories of error especially theory of mis-apprehension (anyathākhyāti) and the doctrine of theory of fruitful activity (saṃvādi-pravṛatti) provide similar evidence but such thinking would be erroneous for, so long as one holds that pramāṇas are exclusively the sources of knowledge ; a theory of error, including 'anyathākhyāti' can have no effect on such a view, only if one conceals the possibility of pramāṇa being a source of error also ; a theory of error would be relevant to the naiure of pramāṇa. Of course one may say that the error is known ab extra but the source of error has nothing to do, accordiug to the official doctrine, with pramāṇa ; the same goes for the doctrine of saṃvādi-pravṛtti. This doctrine only provides a criterion of truth not its definition. The definition of truth as noted above is that a cognition is true if it corresponds to reality. A cognition in virtue of its being true may also lead to utility but this aspect is not part of the essential nature, as it just happens to be the. case. A criterion of truth need not give the nature of truth. So even if one accepts fruitful activity as the criterion of truth one would still be within one's rights in maintaining that truth is what comes from pramāṇa. There would be strictly speaking no tension between the official view of pramāṇa on the one hand and the 'anyathā-khyāti' and 'saṃvādi-pravṛtti-vāda' on the other.

S 4.7. What then is the answer to the question to which we have raised whether the pramāṇas are exclusively sources of knowiedge. As seen above there is evidence for an affirmative answer. There is also evidence for a negative answer. A researcher has to weigh the two types of evidence against each other, and arrive at his conclusion. In the present case there is no doubt that the explicit evidence is right of way for, it indicates that whenever traditional thinkers consciously raised the question their answer was in the affirmative. They might have been wrong in their answers as they indeed were proved to be by the indirect evidence cited above as also by what follows, but that is a different matter. The fact remains, that even as they wanted to give an affirmative answer they did give an affirmative answer. My conclusion is, therefore, that the official answer is on the whole more faithful to the texts. However, the official view is wrong which can be seen from the following consideration.

S 4.8. The view that pramāṇas are exclusively the sources of knowledge is justified retrospectively and, hence. seems to beg the question. On any given occasion when we are called upon to decide whether any pramāṇa is being used at all and if so, which we say that if the concerned cognition turned out to be true then its source is a pramāṇa, otherwise it is something else. We never decide whether something is a pramāṇa independently of the truth value of its product. We decide whether something is a pramāṇa, if so, what is its nature with the help of its product. This procedure of determining the nature of pramāṇa is obviously defective because when the question is raised, as to whether the product is pramā, the answer has to depend upon pramāṇa of the product ; if it is produced by pramāṇa it is pramā but not otherwise.

This kind of circularity is not altogether the same as the kind of circularity referred to earlier (S 3.28). The circularity that was noted earlier and *condoned* was at a conceptual level but the present circularity is at the level of application and is much more objectionable.[9]

S 4.9. The official view that pramāṇas are exclusively the sources of knowledge naturally raises the question about source of false beliefs (apramā). The traditional Indian thinkers are very much conscious of this question and made a determined effort to answer it as could be expected ; but their effort as well as their answer is very awkward. The answer that they have given is that source of false belief is vitiating condition (doṣaḥ).[10] But what is doṣa or defect ? Curiously enough the defect is said to be a defect in one or the other of the pramāṇas.[11] The defect may lie in the subjective mechanism of a pramāṇa, for example, a jaundiced eye, or it may concern the objective conditions involved in knowing an object through a particular pramāṇa, for example, a false belief may arise regarding the size of an object owing to the latter's distance, *i.e.*, a huge object such as the moon appears very small because of its considerable distance from the earth. Similarly a rope perceived in the dusk may appear to be a snake ; the false belief that thus arises is due to the absence of proper light, jaundice, great distance, poor lighting conditions which are also defects concerning perception (pratyakṣābhāsa). Similarly, there are said to be defects in other pramāṇas—anumānābhāsa, upamānābhāsa, śabdābhāsa (āgamābhāsa) etc. In the case of pramāṇas other than perception it is difficult to see how a distinction between subjective defects and objective defects can be maintained. Further in the case of the other pramāṇas the ābhāsās reduce themselves to falsity which is a truth value and, therefore, a property of a cognition. How then can it be a source of false cognition ? To illustrate, "there are hundred elephants on the tip of his finger" is said to be āgamābhāsa but as is obvious it is itself a false cognition, how can it be the source of same false cognition ? Again the so-called hetvābhāsas all turn out to be fallacies of one or the other of the elements of an inference and it is difficult to see how a false element can be the source of false inferential cognition. Same observation can be made about upamānābhāsa also. A further and more serious difficulty is that according to the official doctrine a pramāṇa is by definition correct or free from defects. Therefore, to talk of a defective pramāṇa is self-contradiction. Therefore, to say that a defective pramāṇa is a source of false cognition, hardly makes sense.

The traditional Indian thinkers lead themselves into these oddities because of their view that the pramāṇas are the sources of knowledge only. If they hold, as common sense and contemporary usage do, that pramāṇas are sources of beliefs in general, true as well as false, they could have avoided the oddities.

Notes and References

1. yathābhūtaviṣayakaṃ hi pramāṇamiti. NBh 3.1.51.
2. jñānantu pramāṇajanyaṃ pramāṇañca yathābhūta vastu viṣayakaṃ. SBBS 1,1.4.
3. pramāyogavyavaccinnaṃ pramāṇam. SP 144.
4. avyabhicārinīmasaṁdigdhāmarthopalabdhiṃ. . . pramāṇaṃ. NM 12.
5. yathā pramā jñānasādhāraṇakāraṇabhinnakāraṇa janyā janyajnānatvāt. SM 131,
6. upalabdhisādhanāni pramāṇāni. NBh 1.1.3.
7. anubhūtiscaturvidhā. pratyakṣamapyanumitistatho-pamitiśabdaje. "Experience has four forms; perception, inference, comparison and that due to the (spoken) word." BP 51-2. Translated by Madhavananda 1977:79, 81.

   . . . etāsāṃcatasṛaṇāṃkaraṇāni catvāri pratyakśānumānopamānaśabdāḥ pramāṇāni. The instruments of these four (kinds of knowledge) are to be undersiood as the four mentioned in the aphorism, perception, inference, comparison and verbal testimony are the means. SM 51. Translated by Madhavananda 1977:81,
8. yathārthanubhavakaraṇasyaiva pramāṇatvena vivikṣitatvāt. "For oniy the the instruments of valid experience are intended as means of knowledge." SM 135. Translated by Madhavananda 1977:219. Cf fn 4.1.
9. A possible reply to this objection lines in the fact that the traditional Indian thinkers use perception, inference etc in quite a different way from our own *i.e.*, in ordinary life. Our use of perception overlaps their use of perception and also certain type of apramā, namely, false perception. But I do not see how such a reply can be developed and argued out. It would be arguing at cross purposes and in fact amount to a failure of communication between ourselves and the traditional Indian thinkers. This would be contrary to my purpose which is to make sense of the traditional ideas in terms of contemporary conceptual frame work.
10. doṣoapramāyā janakaḥ. BP 131. Cf VP 148; TD 63; NK 126-7.
11. Vidyabhusana 1971:192-3; Randle 1975:76; Barlingay 1976:15.

5

INDEPENDENCE OF A PRAMĀṆA

S 5.1. Not all systems of Indian philosophy recognise the same number of pramāṇas. In fact there is considerable divergence among the schools regarding the number of pramāṇas recognised. For instance the cārvāka recognises only perception, the Buddhists and the Vaiśeṣikas recognise perception and inference and the Jaina, the Sāṃkhya and the follower of Yoga add one more, *i.e.*, śabda ; the Naiyāyikas add still one more, namely, upamāna raising the number to four. The Prābhākara school of Pūrva-mīmāṃsā includes arthāpatti taking the number to five while the Bhāṭṭa school of Pūrva-mīmāṃsā and Advaita-vedānta add still one more, *i.e.*, anupalabdhi. The number of pramāṇas thus varies from one to six among the different schools. This naturally raises the question what are the criteria used in according to something the status of a pramāṇa. In other words, what makes a pramāṇa unique and independent as against what makes it reducible to some other pramāṇa ? In answer to this question obviously it cannot be found in tracing the common features of all the pramāṇas. It won't help us for instance to say, as the Naiyāyikas do, that all the pramāṇas involve contact of the self with the manas.[1] Nor would it do to say that they are all karṇas instrumental causes), whether we take karaṇa as vyāpāravāda-sādharanaṃ kāraṇam[2] as old Naiyāyikas do[3] ; or as 'phalāyogavyavacchinnaṃ kāraṇam'[4] as Navya-naiyāyikas do.[5] What is needed is a search for the distinct character of an alleged pramāṇa as against that of others and a decision regarding whether that distinctive character is sufficient to give the alleged pramāṇa in question an independent status. The traditional Indian thinkers did pay enough attention to such a search and such a decision. This is evidenced by the fact that they employed various criteria for determining the independent status of a pramāṇa. Some of these deserve consideration here.

S 5.2. One of the criteria sometimes used in the Indian tradition is what is called anuvyavasāya or introspection. In fact Datta (1972 : 339) goes even so far as to say that according to Indian thinkers anuvyavasāya is our chief guide in determining the status of a pramāṇa.[6] For instance the Advaita-vedāntins argue for the independence of upamāna and arthāpatti on the ground that their independence is certified by introspection.[7] Similarly, Annambhaṭṭa is satisfied that testimony is an independent pramāṇa on the ground that it satisfies this criterion of anuvyavasāya.[8]

S 5.3. It does not need much thinking to see that these criteria will not do. To have a convincing feeling without the backing of logical considerations is worse than useless in assessing claim to independence for if two persons claim that they have this convincing feeling about two different alleged pramāṇas it does not follow that the pramāṇas in question are really independent. Again one may have such a feeling on a particular pramāṇa while another may not have it ; how is one to resolve the difference in such a case ? The criterion of anuvyavasāya proves just useless. The Vedāntins may claim introspective certainty about the independence of anupalabdhi but the prābhākaras deny any such certainty; how is then to accept anuvyavasāya as a criterion ? Tne same situation repeats itself in the case of all pramāṇas except perception. So long as 'anuvyavasāya' is not given any logical content it is identified only with the feeling of psychological certitude that it has no epistemological or logical value. Perhaps this was realised at least by some traditional thinkers and that may be the reason why it is treated in a rather lower key. It seems to me that Datta's interpretation which considered 'anuvyavasāya' as a chief guide does not have on the whole sufficient textual backing.

Nor is Datta right (1972 : 339-40), I feel, in holding that 'novelty' is a dependable criterion of independence of pramāṇa. He says ; "For the method to be considered independent it is sufficient that it yields information that is *new* for the *hearer* in that context." For a source may give new knowledge and yet not be considered as a pramāṇa. A Cārvāka, for example, refuses to treat anumāna as independent even though he might agree that it gives new knowledge. As a matter of fact I do not think that the text bears out Datta's interpretation of employment of novelty. Novelty does figure in this regard but it needs to be interpreted in a different way as is indicated below, if thus interpreted it becomes plausible as a criterion.

S 5.4. As a matter of fact novelty itself explicitly used as a criterion of the independence of a pramāṇa in the Indian tradition, is consequential on a explicitly employed criterion. The explicitly used criterion which is also the most plausible of the traditional criteria is what may be called 'the uniqueness of a prameya of a pramāṇa'. It may be formulated thus : "A pramāṇa is independent of, or irreducible to another pramāna if and only if there is at least one object such that that object is known by that particular pramāṇa only and not by any other pramāṇa." In other words, a pramāṇa may be regarded as independent so long as there is at least one object which it alone but no other pramāṇa knows. This of course does not mean that the different pramāṇas cannot be aimed at a common object. In fact a large majority of objects are common to all the pramāṇas, *i.e.*, they can be known by all of them but in the case of each pramāṇa there is at least one object which is the exclusive province of that pramāṇa alone. The Nyāya-bhāṣya (1.1.3) upholds this criterion so emplicitly and emphatically that it is worth quoting what it says in its entirity :

Question :—Have the pramāṇas their objectives in common ? Or is the scope of the pramāṇas restricted within mutually exclusive limits ?

Answer :—As a matter of fact, we find both ways of functioning among pramāṇas. For instance...in the case of fire, we find tnat—(a) when a trustworthy person says 'there is fire at such and such a place', we have the cognition of fire by means of word ; (b) drawing nearer to the place, if we happen to see smoke issuing. we infer from this, the existance of fire :—(c) actually getting at the place, we directly see the fire. On the other hand, in the case of certain

> things we find that one thing is amenable to only one particular pramāṇa ; as for example, that 'the Agnihotra should be performed by one desiring heaven', we can know only by the words of the Veda ; the ordinary man of the world does not know of any indicative features of Heaven (by means of which he could have an inferential cognition) ; nor is he able to *perceive* it directly : similarly when we hear the sound of thunder, from this, we *infer* the source of the sound : and in regard to this we have no perception, nor any verbal cognition ; lastly of our own hand we, have a direct perception, and no Inference or word is operative in this case.[9] Translated by Jha 1939 : 17-8.

Nyāyamanjari (NM : 33) of Jayanta-bhatta fully supports NBh in this regard in all details.

S 5.5. The formulation of a criterion is one thing and its application another. If this criterion of a unique object is to be applied to the different pramāṇas then one has to decide whether in the case of an alleged pramāṇa there is at least one unique object corresponding to it and, if there is, what it is. A pramāṇa is regarded as independent only if one can identify a unique object corresponding to it, and if one cannot identify such an object the pramāṇa in question is not really a pramāṇa but is reducible to something else which is properly a pramāṇa. There can be of course difference of opinion regarding whether a particular object is really a unique object corresponding to a given pramāṇa. It is possible that some people may say that an object O is a unique object concerning a pramāṇa p but other may deny such a claim, and this may happen even when every one concerned may agree that there is at least one unique object concerning the pramāṇa in question. Such a difference of opinion is likely to occur amongst the members of a given school of thought. It may also happen that while some may believe in the existence of a uniqueness of object concerning a given pramāṇa others may not share such abelief. Such a difference of opinion is likely to occur between the members of one school of thought, on the one hand, and those of another school, on the other. Thus the criterion of a unique object may yield a negative result either when there is no agreement regarding the existence of a unique object or when there is no identification of such an object even when it is agreed to exist.[10]

The criterion of a unique object has an important bearing on the question of novelty. If a given pramāṇa is agreed to be independent, the knowledge it gives of its unique object is novel in the sense that it cannot be given by any other pramāṇa. In this sense the criterion of a unique object also amounts to the criterion of novelty. But the epistemic novelty is parasitic on the uniqueness of the known object, and has no independent status. This is why the criterion of novelty as described above may be said to be consequential.

S 5.6. The traditional criterion of the independence of a pramāṇa is then by and large the uniqueness of some of its objects, or what amounts to the same thihg, the novelty of some of its objects. This does not mean that in an actual practice every school of thought applies this criterion explicitly and consciously in resolving the controversies in this regard. We may note here just one regarding postulation (arthāpatti). The Naiyāyikas do not regard arthāpatti as an independent pramāna on the ground that it is reducible to inference (the kevalavyatireki type). The Advaitins on the contrary argue that 'arthāpatti' is an independent pramāṇa mainly on two grounds. The first of these grounds is that introspection (anuvyavasāya) confirms the independence of arthāpatti. The second is that arthāpatti is not reducible to the Advaitins' conception of inference. For the Advaitins kevalavyatireki inference to which, according to Naiyāyikas arthāpatti is reducible, is not at all inference. The Advaitins thus do not dispute the reducibility of arthāpatti to what the Naiyāyikas call kevalavyutiıeki inference but deny to the latter the status of an inference.[11]

S 5.7. It can be seen from this polemics between the Naiyāyikas and the Advaita-vedāntins that the criterion of a uniqueness is used at best indirectly. It can also be seen that a different criterion, namely, confirmation by introspection is also involved. Despite all this when the question is explicitly raised the uniqueness criterion emerges as the strongest candidate. The situation is not much different in the case of anupalabdhi. The Advaitins argue for its independence on the ground (i) that there is no sense-object contact involved in anupalabdhi ; and therefore it is not reducible to perception to which of all the pramāṇas it has the greatest affinity ; (ii) its independence is confirmed by 'anuvyavasāya'. The Naiyāyikas oppose this position of the Advaitins on the ground that it is reducible to perception. For the Naiyāyikas the absence is as much an object as presence and so even in its case the sense-object contact is maintained. Here again the criterion of uniqueness appears indirectly if at all but that does not alter the fact when the question of the criterion of independence is consciously raised the dominant answer given is the criterion of uniqueness. This is not to say that the criterion of uniqueness is not explicitly applied in the case of any pramāṇa. At least in the case of testimony it is explicitly applied to settle the question of its independence. This will be pointed out in great detail later (SS 8.1-8).

Notes and References

1. The Naiyāyikas described the process of perceptual knowledge as follows: The self comes in contact with the mind, the mind with the sense the sense with the object. 'ātmā manasā saṃyujyate, mana indriyeṇa, indriyamartheneti', NBh 1.1.4.

   pratyakṣānumānopamānaśabdānām nimittamātmamanaḥ sanṣnikarah pratyakṣasyaivendriyārthasannikarṣa ityasamānaḥ. "The contact of the mind and of the soul is the (common) cause of perception, as well as inferential, analogical and verbal cognitions; while the contact of the sense-organ with the object is the distinctive cause of perception onl ." NBh. 2.1.26. Translated by Jha 1939:141.

And non-perceptual cognition, however, always involves the contact of the self with the mind.

2. "A peculiar and operative cause (*is instrumental cause*)." Translated by Athalye 1974:184.
3. Athalye 1974:187; NK 200.
4. "A cause, which is invariably and immediately followed by the product." Translated by Athalye 1974:187.
5. Athalye 1974:187; Matilal 1960:66; NK 200.
6. anuvyavasāyaḥ :—yathā ghaṭajñānānantaraṃ ghaṭamahaṃ jānāmi iti mānasa. jñānam NK 35.

   See Datta 1972:339; Chatterjee 1939:339, 385, 394; Bhattacarya 1975:211.

It is not quite clear what exactly "anuvyavasāya' means; it has been taken to be apperception by Satprakasananda (1974:155;160) and Madhavananda (1972:85; 122); and as introspection by Datta (1972:339); Chatterjee (1939:339, 385, 394) and C. Bhattacarya (1975:211). While the terms "apperception", "introspection" have a certain affinity; apperception seems to be wider in scope and more general in character than "introspection." "Anuvyavasāya" seems to be closer to introspection. But there is an etymological difficulty here; "anuvyavasāya" literally means "*after cognition*" but introspection is the concurrent cognition of cognition. Obviously an after cognition and a *concurrent cognition* are incompatible. This difficulty is resolved by saying that 'anuvyavasāya' is introspection of the memory of a cognition (c), not of 'C' itself; since the memory of C is after cognition of C and since the introspection of that memory is a concurrent cognition of the memory of C, it follows that 'anuvyavasāya' is both an after cognition and a concurrent cognition and that there is no real inconsistency in being both at the same time. (See Datta 1972:339).

7. anena sadṛśī madīyā gauḥ iti pratīteranubhavasiddhatvāt, upaminomi ityanuvyavasāyācca. VP 84. Cf Vidyabhusana 1971:444.

   at a evārthāpattisthale 'anuminomi' iti nānuvyavasāyaḥ, kintu anena idaṃ kalpayāmi iti. VP 122.

8. śābdajñānasya vilakṣaṇasya śabdātpratyemītyanuvyasāyasākśikasya sarvasaṃatatvāt. TD 63. Cf Vidyabhusana 1971:445; Bhattacarya 1975:211.

9. kiṃ punaḥ pramāṇāni prameyamabhisaṃplavanteatha pratiprameyaṃ vyavatisthante iti ? ubhayathā darśanam . . . agnirātopadeśātpratīyate 'atrāgniḥ' iti. pratyāsīdatā dhūmadarśanenānumīyate, pratyāsannena ca pratyakśata upalabhyate. vyavasthā punaḥ :—'agnihotraṃ juhuyātsvargakāmaḥ' iti. laukikasya svarge na lingadarśanna pratyaksam. stanayitnuśabde śrūyamāṇe śabdahetoranumānam. tatra na pratyakṣannāgamaḥ pāṇau pratyakṣat upalabhyammāne nānumānannāgamā iti. NBh 1.1.3.

10. The position of Śaṇkara on the uniqueness criterion is unclear; on the one hand, there are passages such as the following :

    na ca pramāṇaṃ pramāṇantareṇa virudhyate. pramāntarāviṣayameva hi pramāṇantaram jñāpayati. "And one means of knowledge does not contradict another, for it only tells about those things that cannot be known by any other means." SBBU 2.1.20. Translated by Madhavananda 1975:209.

    tat brahma sarvajñam sarvaśakti jagadutpatti sthitilayakāraṇaṃ vedāntaśāstradevāvagamyate. "Tat (That) means Brahman, which is omniscient and omnipotent, which is the cause of the origin, existence, and dissolution of the universe, and which is known as such from the upaniṣads (*śruti*) alone." SBBS 1.1.4. Translated by Gambhirananda 1972:21.

On the other hand, there are also passages which seem to discredit it and to argue for tne convergence of all pramāṇas. Consider for instance the following passage :

yadvi pratyakśadīnamanyatamena pramāṇenopalabhpyate tatsambhavati... iha tu sarvaireva pramaṇairbahyoartha upalabhyamānaḥ. "What is known though any one of the means of knowledge, such as direct percep- etc., is possible. . . In the case under discussion, the external things are known individually by the respective means of knowledge." SBBS 2.2 28. Translated by Gambhirananda 1972:420.

However contextually the position of Śaṅkara is that there are common objects (prameyas) which are known by, more than one pramāṇas; and unique objects can be known only by their respective pramāṇas so that with respect to a certain object there is no convergence of pramāṇas. SBBS 1.1.4 ; S 8.7.

11. For further details on the question of independence or otherwise of arthā patti, please see VP 73-4. 122-4; BP 144; SM 144; TD 63.

6

ŚABDA-PRAMĀṆA

S 6.1. The word śabda is translated as speech by some for example Vidyabhusana (1971 : 444) : Keith (1977 : 158, 165) and as word by some others for example Athalye (1974 : 329) ; C. Bhattacharya (1975 : 17, 197). But these translations are obviously inadequate for, śabda as a pramāṇa is a source of knowledge and the unit of knowledge is a thought which in turn is expressed by a statement ; so "testimony" would be an apter rendering ; I have, therefore, followed it in this thesis. Some times the word 'authority' is also used as a synonym for 'śabda'[1], but this again is not altogether correct because as it is shown below (S 6.2) all testimony need not be authoritative.[2]

S 6.2. Śabda is defined by Gautama as 'āptopadeśaḥ', *i.e.*, as a statement of a trustworthy person (NS 1.1.7), Annaṃbhaṭṭa practically repeats the same : 'āptavākyaṃ śabdaḥ' ; "Testimony is a statement of a trustworthy person (TS 59). But who is an āpta or a trustworthy person ? An āpta is sometimes decribed as an authoritative person[3] or a person having expert knowledge in a given field. But such a description would be wrong for a trustworthy person need not be an expert ; to consider an example, one may ask in a strange place a strange person about correct facts to reach one's destination and the stronger may correctly give the information but his doing so can be hardly called expertise as this term is ordinarily used.[4] Perhaps this is brought out by Vātsyāyana's formulation of the criteria of an āpta. These are (i) possession of relevant knowledge (ii) integrity of motivation and (iii) ability for adequate communication.[5] The first requirement does not necessarily make a person an expert because the knowledge involved might be just ordinary knowlege and not a specialised or expert knowledge.[6] One can easily see, the second requirement is quite independent of the expertise. A man of integrity need not be an expert. Similar is the case regarding the ability to communicate adequately ; what is communicated need not be specialised or expert knowledge.

Nor is there any suggestion of expertise in Annaṃbhaṭṭa's characteristisation of an āpta, namely, that an āpta is a speaker of truth.[7] The truth which an āpta tells need not concern any specialised field or be an expertise, it may just be an ordinary truth. 'Āpta' is, therefore, best understood as a trustworthy or reliable person than as an authority or an expert. A trustworthy person is a reliable person and not necessarily an expert. Essentially, therefore, an āpta is a man of integrity, *i.e.*, a trustworty person.

S 6.3. It may be noted that the Naiyāyikas do not confine the term 'āpta' to human beings, they distinguish between two kinds of testimony, namely, mundane (laukika) and scriptural (alaukika or vaidika)[8], and both of them are regarded as 'āpta vacanas', *i.e.*, 'āpta vākyas' even though the word 'āpta' does not figure in the explicit characterisation of scriptural testimony. They say that scriptural testimony is what is uttered by Īśvara while mundane testimony is what is uttered by a trustworthy person.[9] This seems to give the impression that an āpta is necessarily a human being but I do not think such an impression is justified for the general characterisation of śabda of which both laukika and vaidika variety of forms, is that it is āptavākyaṃ, in other words even vaidika śabda is a form of āptavākyaṃ. This gains support from the fact that even īśvara is considered as an āpta by the Naiyāyikas.[10]

S 6.4. Like the Naiyāyikas the Advaita-vedāntins (and the Bhāṭṭas) also regard testimony as 'āpta vacana', *i.e.*, statement of trustworthy person (Satprakasananda 1974 : 173, 189-90). They also distinguish between two forms of testimony, namely, pauruṣeya (human), *i.e.*, laukika and apauruṣeya (authorless), *i.e.*, alaukika[11] (Satprakasananda 1974 : 193). However, these two forms do not altogether coincide with the two forms accepted by the Naiyāyikas, even though some use the same pairs of terms, namely, "laukika" and "alaukika" to describe them (Satprakasananda 1974 : 193). But the difference between the two schools is insubstantial. It is simply that for the Naiyāyikas alaukika śabda also is pauruṣeya in as much as the scriptures are authored by God, and God for them is a puruṣa or a person ; while for the Advaitins and the Bhāṭṭas the scriptures are authorless and hence apauruṣeya.

S 6.5. Again, just as there is an *apparent* inconsistency in the Nyāya conception of the distinction of the two kinds of testimony (S 6.3), there is also a similar *apparent* inconsistency in the Vedānta (and the Bhāṭṭa) conception of the two fold distinction. They also, while regarding śabda in general as āptavacana (S 6.4), yet explicitly confine the word 'āpta' to pauruṣeya śabda[12]. (Human testimony for them is āpta vacana) while authorless testimony is scriptural. But the inconsistency is once again only apparent. The scriptures, though apauruṣeya are yet the sources of truth (and of the highest truth at that) and therefore, qualify as āpta. We may then conclude that essentially testimony is the statement of a trustworthy source (human or otherwise) for all the three schools, namely, Nyāya, Advaita and Bhāṭṭā.

S 6.6. It is seen from the foregoing consideration that the concept of an āpta is very essential to the concept of śabda pramāṇa or testimony and it is perhaps this reason that Vātsyāyana explicitly enunciates the criteria of an āpta as noted above (S 6.2). The three criteria are (i) possession of direct knowledge, (ii) integrity of motivation and (iii) ability to communicate adequately. It is worthwhile, in view of the importance of the concept to elaborate a little more on these criteria.

S 6.7. (i) *Possession af direct knowledge.* That a trustworthy source is well informed, *i.e.*, has the relevant knowledge is trivially true ; but must the knowledge, such a trustworthy source possesses be direct as required by Vātsyāyana, that it need not be so is realised by Jayanta-bhaṭṭa. Jayanta-bhaṭṭa says the knowledge may be even indirect (inferential).[13] In fact the question of whether the knowledge in question is direct or indirect is beside the point. What is important and necessary is that the knowledge that the trustworthy source has must be relevant, *i.e.*, must be about the subject at hand. In fact, it is even that this possible relevant knowledge should itself have come from another āpta, this means that an āpta is a relative source ; a source may be an āpta for me but not for you. This relativity is consistent with Vātsyāyana's first criterion. That trustworthy person has a relevant knowledge obviously carries an implication, which according to Jayanta-bhaṭṭa is that an āpta must be free from delusion.[14]

S 6.8. (ii) *Integrity of motivation.* This criterion eliminates cheats and fraudulent persons. A person who knowingly tells a falsehood with a view to misleading the listener for whatever reasons can never qualify himself to be an āpta. This again seems to be trivial ; a trustworthy person by definition is one whose motives are above suspicion. How can a person whose motives are known to be suspect be regarded as reliable ? It may of course happen that a person A may fall a prey to a mischievous motive of a person B and may take the latter as an āpta. But when A begins to act on B's words he is sure to discover sooner or later that B has misled him perhaps deliberately. And as soon as such a discovery is made, the status of āpta accorded to B by A stands annulled by A. It it to be noted that integrity of motive is quite distinct from expertise, this was remarked earlier (S 6.2) and will be developed further (S 6.11). It implies as Vātsyāyana points out a desire to help one's fellow beings and not to harm or milead them.[15]

S 5.9. (iii) *Ability to commuuicate adequately.* Jayanta-bhaṭṭa explains the point of this criterion, by saying that a dumb person cannot be an āpta even though he possesses the relevant knowledge ; that is because he lacks the ability for adequate communication (NM 138). He can of course communicate through gestures but, it can hardly be counted as adequate communication. However, this is too general a requirement for one may be very good at communication and yet be a villain, *i.e.*, be far from an āpta.

S 6.10. Montague (1958 : 41-5) considers three criteria of what he calls authority (=expert testimony), namely, prestige, number and age. Of these three he himself rejects the latter two. Just because a person has large number of followers does uot mean that his statements are reliable. One may fool a large number of people and get away with it. Similarly, Montague argues just because a certain statement has been accepted over the centuries it does not necessarily become reliable. However, Montague's first criterion, namely, prestige combines Vātsyāyana's first and second criteria, *i.e.*, if a person is both intellectually competent in the given area and is also known for his integrity of charaeter then his statements surely become reliable.

S 6.11. How do we know which person is an āpta ? As noticed above an āpta may be an expert or a non-expert. The present question, namely; how do we know which person is an āpta, is perhaps easily answered with respect to an expert. It might be thought that we have to simply employ the three criteria enumerated above to locate or identify an āpta. But such an impression would be really wrong for the difficulty that is initially felt regarding how does one know who is an āpta is now shifted backwards to the level of the application of the criteria themselves, Now we have to ask how do we know that an alleged āpta has the relevant knowledge ; how do we know that a person is a man of integrity ; how do we know that a man has ability for adequate communication. To all these questions the answer is substantially the same namely, "on the basis of past experience." And the same answer could be given to the initial question, namely, how do we know who is an (expert) āpta ? Whether a person possesses expert and relevant knowledge in the given area can be known mostly by past expcrienee about the given person ; he has proved his competence in appropriate context either to my own satisfaction or to the satisfaction of those well qualified to judge his claims in whom I have faith. The latter case indicates that the identification of an expert might itself involve the recourse to testimony and this is an unending process. The questions about integrity and ability to communicate are not as important as the question of the possession of relevant and adequate knowledge in the area. But they are also answered similarly; namely, on the basis of past experience. In saying that we know that some one is morally and intellectually qualified inductively; I am not alone for example Price's (1969 : 114, 116-7) principle of testimony also says the same thing : what there is said to be there is more often than not.

It might be suggested that the qnestion of 'how we know that some one is a non-expert 'āpta' is similarly settled. This is not so for a non-expert āpta may be a total stranger as was earlier illustrated (S 6.2).[16] In such cases the question of relying on past experience does not just arise. How then is one to decide whether a given person is non-expert āpta ? The answer given to this question by the traditional Indian thinkers is that we accept a non-expert as an āpta if we do not have any reason to distrust him (NM 153). Thus even a stranger can be called an āpta so long as there is no basis for questioning his reliability.

S 6.12. In traditional logic appeal to authority (testimony) is recognised as a fallacy (fallacy of vericundium). But from what is said above it is clear that not all appeals to authority are fallacious. For example, appeals to authority based on what Montague calls criteria of age and number may be fallacious, but appeals to authority based on what he calls prestige are not (Copi 1972 : 80-1). While the inference

x asserts p,
∴ p

is clearly unsound, the inference

x who is accepted as reliable in the relevant field asserts p,

∴ p,

is not. The latter inference is of course not deductively valid but inductively quite adequate (Salmon 1973 : 91-2).

Notes and References

1. Datta 1972:336; Masilal 1977:420-1; Potter 1977:176, 406.
2. The word testimony is also used in other senses for instance in the sense of witness (Russel 1951 b to 206).
3. Potter 1977:176,406; Athalye 1974:329; Chatterjee 1939:381.
4. For traditional example, see Radhakrishnan 1977b:110; Chatterjee 1939 : 322-3.
5. āptaḥ khalu sākṣātkṛtadharmā yathādṛṣtasyārthasya cikhyāpayiṣıyā prayukta upadeṣṭā. "That person is called 'āpta'. 'reliable,' who possesses the direct and right knowledge of things, who is moved by a desire to to make known (to others) the thing as he knows it, and who is fully capable of speaking of it." NBh 1.1.7: Translated by Jha 1939:30. Cf NBh 2.1.69; NM 138.
6. ṛṣyāryamlechhānaṃ samānaṃ lakṣaṇaṃ. "This definition applies to sages as well as to Āryas and Mlecchas." NBh 1.1.7. Translated by Jha 1939:30. Cf NM 138.
7. āptastu yathārthavaktā. TS 59.

8. āptavākyaṃ śabdaḥ. . .vākyaṃ dvividham. vaidikam laukikaṃ ca. TS 59,62.
9. vaidikamīśvaroktatvātsarvameva pramāṇam. laukikaṃ tvāptoktaṃ pramāṇam. TS 62.
10. āptaṃ tameva bhagavantamanādimīśamāśritya viśvāsiti vedavacassu lokaḥ. "All persons pin their faith in the words of the vedas because they believe that vedas have been composed by eternal and trustworthy God who is possessed of all excellent virtues." NM 220. Translated by J.V. Bhattacharya 1978:499. āptaprāmāṇyācca prāmāṇyam. laukikeṣu śabdeṣu caitatsamānamiti, ". . .if we attribute the trustworthiness of words to the trustworthiness of the veracious expositor, it meets the case of vedic as well as ordinary words." NBh 2.1.69; Translated by Jha 1939:194.
11. .. pauruṣeyāpauruṣeyabhedena dividha āgamonirūpitaḥ. ". . .two kinds of verbal testimony have been determiued *viz.*, that which is connected with a person and that which is not." VP 115. Translated by Madhavananda 1972:116, MN 105.
12. lankikānāmapi maṇimantrauṣadhiprabhratīnāṃ deśakālanimittavaicitryavaśāchchaktayo viruddhānekakāryaviṣayā dṛśyante. tā api tāvannopadeśamantareṇa kevalena tarkeṇāvagnatuṃ śakyante—asya vastuna etāvatya estatsahāyā etatdviṣayā etatprayojanāśca śaktya iti. "Even the things of this world like jems, incantations, herbs, and so on, are seen to possess many powers capable of producing incompatible effects under the influence of a variety of space (eovironment), time, and cause. And even these powers can be known not from mere reasoning but from such instruction as, "such a thing has such kinds of potency with the aid of such things, on such things, and for such purposes." SBBS 2.1.27. Translated by Gambhirananda 1972:355. Hiriyanna 1973:358; MN 105.
13. na tu pratyakṣeṇaiva gṛhaṇamiti niyamaḥ anumānādiniscitārthopadeśinoapyāptatvanapāyāt. "There is no hard and fast rule that the subject-matter of his teaching is to be intuited since an inferred matter may also be taught." NM 138. Translated by J. Bhattacharya 1978:315.
14. yeapyātiṃ doṣayamācakśate tairapi doṣakśayaḥ pratipādhyārtheṣveva varṇanīyoanyathā loke dṛśyamānasyātoktinibandhasya vyavahārasya nihnāvaḥ. ". . ,the essence of an āpta lies in the freedom from such defects as are error, inadvertence, etc., and a man having on such defects, is an āpta. . ." NM. 138 Translated by J. Bhattacharya 1978:316.
15. āptāḥ. . .bhūtanyanukampante—teṣāṃ khalu vai prānabhṛtāṃ svayamanavabudhyamānāmnyadupadeśādvabodhakaraṇamasti. na cānavabodhe samīhā varjanaṃ vā, na vāartvā vastibhvāaḥ, nāpyasyānya upakārakoapyasti. . . "Veravious persons . . . take compassion on living beings, that is they feel as follows : 'These poor creatures being by themselves ignorant, there is no other means save instruction, available to them for knowing things; until they know, they cannot either perform or avoid any acts, and unless they do perform acts, it cannot be will with them, and there is no one (save myself) who would help them in this matter. . ." NBh 2.1.69. Translated by Jha 1939:192.
16. It may be noted that an expert author cannot be a stranger for the fact that he is accepted as an expert āpta implies that he has been already answered directly or indirectly.

7

VAIDIKA ŚABDA

S 7.1 It is earlier noticed (SS 6.3-4) that there are two kinds of testimony, namely, mundane testimony (laukika śabda) and scriptural testimony (alaukika śabda). The nature of mundane testimony is obvious enough and is brought out in the course of our discussion of the nature of testimony in general, it, therefore, does not need any special treatment. However, scriptural testimony does need a special treatment because it does involve certain points which are far from obvious or straightforward.

S 7.2 what then is scriptural testimony ? The answer given to this question is that it is the Veda. But this answer is not of much help, because the word Veda is ambiguous. As Bloomfield (1972;17) points out the word Veda is used in two ways, namely,(i) as collective designation of the entire sacred literature of India, (ii) as a specific designation of a single work belonging to that literature. It is clear that the second is the narrower of the two senses and it is in this sense that we speak of the four vadas, namely, Ṛg, Yajur, Sāma and Atharva. In the wider sense (i) the Veda comprises : (i) śruti (what is heard as a sacred word), (2) smṛti (what is remembered as a sacred word), (3) itihāsa (historical treatise), and (4) purāṇa (mythological treatise).

S 7.3 Of these four types of literature each preceding type is presumed to be of higher authority than the succeeding one. Thus śruti is of the highest authority and purāṇas are the lowest.

(1) Śruti :—It is just the Veda in the second or the narrower sense and comprises Ṛg—Veda, Yajur—Veda, Sāma—Veda and Atharva—Veda. Each of these four Vedas is divided into four parts, namely, the Saṃhitā (collection of hymna), Brāhmaṇas (ritualistic treatises), Āraṇyakas (forest treatises) and Upaniṣads (philosophical treatises).

(2) Smṛti :—It comprises a variety of works on religious duties and philosophy (for example Manusmṛti), while it is not the same as śruti it nevertheless draws its inspiration from the Vedas proper as the final authority. Smṛti becomes an authority only when śruti is silent on a given question and only when it is nor inconsistent with śruti.[1]

(3) Itihāsa :—These are the two great epics, the Rāmāyaṇa and the Mahābhārata. They recount the noble deeds of the great heroes and are illustrative of the laws of smṛti.

(4) Purāṇas :—Though these are mythological works they embody religious knowledge and evoke religious devotion among the masses. They employ the medium of myths parables, legends etc.[2]

S 7.4 When scriptural testimony is said to be just the Veda, what is intended is that the Veda proper is śruti which comprises the four Vedas with their four-fold division. Of course different schools emphasis different parts of the Veda in the sense when they talk about scriptural testimony for example the Mīmāṃsakas emphasise the Saṃhitās and the Brāhmaṇas.[3] The Naiyāyikas emphasise the Brāhmaṇas (NBh 2.1.13). The Advaita-Vedāntins on the other hand, emphasise especially the Upaniṣadic part (Satprakasananda 1974:218). These differering emphasis by different schools on the different portions of the śruti correspond to another division of the Veda into karmakāṇḍa which comprises the Saṃhitās and the Brāhmaṇas, and the jñāna-kāṇḍa which comprises especially the Upaniṣads. Mahadevan (1971:31) prefers to divide the Veda into three divisions rather than two, namely; (a) ritual section (karma-kāṇḍa), (b) meditation section (upāsana-kāṇḍa), and (c) knowledge section (jñānā-kāṇḍa). He treats Āraṇyaka portion as Upāsana-kāṇḍa and the Upaniṣadic portion as jñāna-kāṇḍa. The Āraṇyakas for him are neither purely ritualistic nor purely philosophical, but occupy a midway position.

S 7.5 In view of the fact that scriptural testimony is identical with the Veda, it will be helpful to consider in some detail the general characteristics of the four parts of the Veda. This is what I proceed to do below in brief.

(i) The Saṃhitās :—There are four collections of hymns, namely, Ṛg-Veda Saṃhitā, Sāma-veda Saṃhitā, Yajurveda Saṃhitā and Atharva-veda Saṃhitā. These Saṃhitās contain the super human sacred knowledge in the forms of hymns, prayers and ritual formulas.

(ii) The Brāhmaṇas :— These theological treatises grew up after the saṃhitās, wnich are of distinctly different types of literature. These works are the commentaries on Saṃhitā written in prose and explain the significance of the different rituals. It is believed that they reflect the spirit of an age in which the entire intellectual activity is focussed on the sacrifice, explaining its ceremonies etc.

(iii) The Āraṇyakas :—These forest treatises form the transitional connection between the Bṛāhmaṇas, and the Upaniṣads. The main aim of the Ārnayakas is to serve as objects of meditation for those who live in forests. The difference between the Brāhmaṇas and the Āraṇyakas is on account of the fact that the former deal with the procedure of ritual to be practiced by the householder whereas the latter serve as guiding literature concerning the techniques of meditations for those who live in the forests. These treatises discuss the symbolic and spiritual aspects of the sacrificial cult in the process of meditation.

(iv) The Upaniṣads :—These philosophical treatises form the concluding portions of the Veda. As they come at the end of the Veda, they are also called the Vedānta and form the basis for most of the latter philosophies and religions. The discussions in these texts are mainly centered around the nature of Ātman and Brahman.

For a classified list of the Vedic texts see Satprakasananda (1974:309-10); Radhakrishnan (1977a:65).

S 7.6 Scriptural testimony as noticed above is identical with the Veda. But one of the questions that figures prominently in the traditional literature concerning the Veda, is whether it is authorless (apauruṣeya) or whether it has an author (pauruṣeya). The Mīmāṃsakas and the Naiyāyikas are in opposite camps on this issues and the Advaitins seem to be trying for a compromise between the two schools (Athalye 1974:356; Murty 1974:45). I shall first consider the two opposite views and then the compromised view.

S 7.7 The Mīmāṃsaka theory :—The Mīmāṃsakas are known for their view that the Veda is eternal and cannot be considered to have an author. They give several arguments for their view. The more important arguments are given below.

S 7.8 (i) Tradition does not mention any authors for the Ṛṣis cannot be said to be the authors of the Veda, being merely the seers of the hymns (ṛṣiḥmantradraṣṭā)[4] but they are not composers. The weakness of this argument is obvious: just because no autoor is mentioned anywhere, it does not follow that the work is authorless. Though the argument is not conclusive it still provides a corroborative evidence for Mīmāṃsakas' view.[5]

S 7.9 (ii) The Vedas themselves declare their own eternity in many texts. For example, Bṛhadāraṇyakaupaniṣad says that Ṛg-Veda, Yajur-Veda, Sāma-Veda, Atharva-Veda are (like) the breath of this infinite Reality.[6] This argument again will not do just because a composition claims to be eternal, it does not follow that it is indeed eternal. It is a matter of common experience that many compositions make false claims and sometimes even get away with it. The question, therefore, still remains whether the claim is valid. This argument thus is even weaker than the first; it does not provide even a corroborative feature.

S 7.10 (iii) Another argument is that there is this beginningless tradition of vedic study and things would not be possible if the Veda were not eternal (NM 214). This argument also will not do, for, it involves the factual claim that the Vedic study is beginningless and the claim is, to say the least, questionable. In fact the Naiyāyikas are quick to question it and point out that the tradition of the Vedic study does have beginning (NM 214).

S 7.11 (iv) The most important Mīmāṃsakas' argument however, for the eternity of the Veda is to be found in their account of varṇa and dhvani (Hiriyanna 1973:310). A varṇa is simply a member of the Sanskrit alphabet like 'ga', a dhvani is a tone or sound through the medium of which a varṇa is uttered. A varṇa according to the Mīmāṃsakas is eternal and they stick to this view tenaciously even in the face of strong objections.[7] These objections come especially from the Naiyāyikas who hold that a varṇa comes into being when it is uttered nor written down) and ceases to be when it is neither uttered nor written.[8] The Mīmāṃsakas' reply to such an objection is that a varṇa cannot come into being when it is uttered for in that case the varṇa 'ga' uttered by me and varṇa 'ga' uttered by you would be different from each other. The truth according to Mīmāṃsaka is that, a varṇa is simply manifested when uttered or written and not brought into being; it still exists even when it is not menifested and as a fact it is ever existing.[9]

While the Mīmāṃsaka is right in exposing the weakness of the Nyāya position still he is not right in saying that a varṇa is eternal. His criticism of the Nyāya position reminds us of the contemporary type-token distinction. A type can remain the same in the face of differing tokens, the different utterances of varṇa 'ga' are tokens of the same type, namely, the varṇa 'ga'. There is a sense in saying that the transitariness of the differing tokens does not affect the self-identity of which are the tokens but this does not mean that the type is eternal as the Mīmāṃsaka maintains; it may be eternal but even if it were so it does not follow from the transitariness of the tokens.

S 7.12 A word (pada or śabda)[10] is a collection of varṇas, this would seem to make every word also eternal; but, however, this is not so according to the Mīmāṃsaka for a word also involves a certain order of the varṇas and this order need not be eternal. For if it were so, every word would be eternal and so every statement including false ones and every type of literature would be eternal and this is contrary to facts. How then is the Veda eternal ?

S 7.13 The Veda is said to be eternal because in its case the order of varṇas alone is eternal, according to Mīmāṃsakas. Such an order is not eternal in case of other expositions and that is why they are non-eternal inspite of the fact that varṇas are eternal. But in the cass of Veda the order (ānupūrvī) and the elements *i.e.*, the varṇas both equally participate in eternality.

S 7.14 Not only do the Mīmāṃsakas hold that the varṇas are eternal but also they are credited to the view that the relation between a word and its meaning (artha) is eternal or natural, in other words they are supposed to have maintained that a word comes to have a certain meaning because of its very nature. Just as there is the natural relationship between smoke and fire; so also it is contended that there is natural relationship between word and meaning.[11] Such a view then would entail certain consequences which probably would not be accepted by Mīmāṃsakas themselves. Some of these are : (i) on such a view not only varṇas but also words have to be eternal. This would mean all literary compositions including false statements would be eternal; (ii) the same word would always have the same meaning and ambiguity of meaning would be self-contradiction. (iii) on such a view a plurality of languages would have to be ruled out and language would not admit any change. Neither the introduction of new symbols nor the rejection of the existing symbols nor even the modification of existing symbols would be permissible.

S 7.15. The view that language is the system of conventional signs is so well established now that it hardly needs to be argued out. The only explanation as to why the Mīmāmsakas accepted such a patently false thesis is that it implies the eternity of the Veda. But that is a very dubitable advantage. Authors like Raja (1969:20) try to mitigate the absurdity of this view by saying that what really means is that, as far as our knowledge goes, words had always their meaning and that their meaningfuiness cannot be traced to any human being. Even if such a charitable interpretation of the Mīmāṃsakas' naturalism were true it is not clear how it goes against the conventionalism of language; and it is in fact not true, for there is such a thing as the introduction of new words in a language and when this happens a particular person becomes the author of a particular meaning of word, compare for example "The category mistake" of G. Ryle, "Logical atomism" of Russell, Leibniz's "Monads", "The Dasein" of Kierkegaard. There is such a thing as stipulative definition according to which unmeaningful symbols are constantly introduced and given fresh meanings. This is how highly technical terms in the frontier areas of knowledge acquire meaning.

S 7.16 Some other authors, for example, Hiriyanna (1973:311) would interpret naturalism so as not to exclude conventionalism. Still others, for example, Jayanta Bhatta (NM 222) (Bhattacharya 1977:505) would seem to allow ambiguity and diversity for the same symbol within the framework of Mīmāsakas' naturalism. But such attempts make the Mīmāṃsakas' naturalism self-contradictory and thus really destroy its character altogether.

S 7.17 The Mīmāṃsakas' naturalism of course entails the eternity of the Veda but gives the impression that it is specially manufactured just for that purpose. No thesis can be established by arguments which are tailored for that purpose, which do not have any plausibility independently of that purpose. The cogency of an argument depends not only on its logic but also on the truth of its premisses, and on this latter ground the Mīmāṃsakas' naturalism can only be said to be very hollow.[12]

S 7.18 (v) It is a necessary consequence of authorship that what is authored has some defect or falsity. On the other hand, Vedic statements, being intrinsically true and free from all defects, cannot hence be authored and the Veda can only be eternal. Of course, this argument is untenable because according to the apauruṣeyavādins like Mīmāṃsakas and Advaita-vedāntins the truth of true statement (not necessarily vedic statement) is intrinsic to it and yet does not follow that it is authorless. It is a triviality that the most ordinary statements which are true are authored.

S 7.19 The Nyāya theory :—The Naiyāyikas in opposition to Mīmāṃsakas maintain that the Veda has an author and that is God himself.[13] The chief among their arguments for this view are the following :—

S 7.20 (i) The Veda itself declares that it is authored by God.[14] This argument is in immediate contrast with the Mīmāṃsakas' argument (ii) stated above. The criticism that I made against Mīmāṃsakas' argument applies almost exactly to the argument of the Naiyāyikas as well. When opposite views are held on the same issue, the issue has to be settled independently and the possibility of the divine authorship of the Veda claimed by the Naiyāyikas cannot be allowed until the issue is independently settled, the claim cannot justify itself.

The Mīmāṃsakas have an interesting criticism against this argument : "It it is held that the Vedas themselves declare that God is the author of them then it is a case of circular reasoning. The Vedas are the sources of true knowledge because God is their author. Again, we known that God is their author since the Vedas are the source of knowledge."[13] In other words, the Mīmāṃsakas accused the Naiyāyikas of circular argument. The Naiyāyikas wriggle out of this charge by a clever but a plausible device. They point out that the knowledge of God is obtained not necessarily through the Veda, it is also obtained independently of it (scriptural testimony) *i.e.*, by inference. They employ the argument from the design : Just as we infer about the existence of a weaver on the basis of the observation of this product, namely, cloth; we could also infer about the existence of the author of the Veda *i.e.*, God from the systematic arrangement of words in the form of the Veda.[16]

S 7.21 (ii) A varṇa is not eternal because it comes into being and ceases to be when not uttered (fn 7.8). As noted above (S 7.11) Mīmāṃsakas criticise this argument with a view to establishing the eternality of the Veda; while their conclusion does not follow; the Naiyāyikas' argument also is not without fault as it stands, for if every varṇa comes into being when uttered then the varṇa 'ga' uttered by me would be different from the same uttered by you (S 7.11). However, their fault can be easily remedied and Nyāya argument may be modified to the effect that the varṇa as a type comes into being and passes out of being, and 'that this is attested overhelmingly by experience. That the Naiyāyikas are right is now a common place, thanks to linguistic studies for the past several decades.

S 7.22 (iii) It is generally accepted view that every well formed statement must have four properties; expectancy (ākāṅkṣā), competancy (yogyatā), proximity (saṁnidhi) and intention (tātparya).[17] So these properties must also belong to the Vedic statements and the intention that belongs to them cannot be that of any ordinary speaker or author; in view of the profundity of the truths expressed, it can only be that of God. Hence the author of the Veda must be God.[18]

This argument is defective for several reasons : (i) where intention is spoken of as a property of a well formed statement, what is obviously meant is the sense of that statement or expression in general and not intention (in the psychological sense) of any given utterer. If intention were taken in the psychological sense we should be able to infer from the sense of the given statement its author. But this we cannot do always. This is so because the sense of an expression is something independent of its utterer and has to be determined without reference to the author. As a matter of fact the psychological associations that arise in the minds of the utterer on the occasion of uttering to express are irrelevant to the sense of that expression. The Naiyāyikas are interpreting intention not in their logical sense of "sense" but in the psychological sense of intending. In this they are clearly wrong; and their conclusion, therefore, the divine authorship of the Veda based on this consideration is untenable.

S 7.23 (iv) According to Naiyāyikas' account of utpattivāda (S 11.4) what gives rise to a true cognition is the excellence (guṇa) of its causal conditions. The Vedic statements are all true and, therefore, must have merits or excellence of their causal conditions. But if they were authorless such a condition would not be accountable and in view of the unique subject-matter their author could only be the supreme being.

This argument is obviously unsound because it assumes without proof that Vedic statements are all true but if asked why they are all true the implied Naiyāyikas' answer is that, because they are authored by God, in other words the truth of Vedic statements is not established independently of reference to God when the authorship of the Veda itself is in question, the reference to God in establishing the validity of Vedic statements amounts to begging the question.

S 7.24 Advaita theory :—As remarked above (S 7.6) the Advaita theory on the question of the authorship or ortherwise of the Veda is a compromise between the diametrically opposite theories of Nyāya and Mīmāṃsaka. According to Advaita-vedānta there are cycles of creation and destruction of the universe, each cycle comes into being and passes out of being. At the beginning of each cycle of creation Īśvara produces the same Veda,[19] which means that the Veda is apauruṣeya and eternal. On this point there are different views and it is worthwhile to consider some of them here.

S 7.25 (i) S. Murthy (1974;49-50) maintains that the Veda is non-eternal on the ground that it is produced by Īśvara in each kalpa. He also says that it is apauruṣeya on the ground that Īśvara reproduces it in each kalpa. He does not produce something new but what was already existing in the preceding kalpas. He bases his view on Vedānta-paribhāṣā.

(ii) Athalye (1974:346) holds that while contents of the Veda are eternal, its form (ānupūrvī) is non-eternal, in the sense that it may vary with a cosmic cycle. Strangely enough Athalye also says that the Veda of each kalpa is merely a copy of the Vedas of the previous kalpas. But if this were so it is not clear how the form or the order of the Veda varies with different kalpas. One would have thought that all copies are of the same form. Despite this difficulty Athalye like Murty seems to regard the Veda non-eternal and authorless. It must be noted that Athalye also bases his view on Vedānta-paribhāṣa.

(iii) Satprakasananda (1974:217-18) maintains on the basis of both VP (115) and SBBU (2.4.10) that the Veda is both without beginning and without end; it is revealed by Īśvara but anew. It is, therefore, authorless (apauruṣeya) in the sense that Īśvara has no freedom in its composition. Though Satprakasanda is silent on whether it is content or the form (or both) that is eternal, the implication seems to be the Veda is eternal, regarding to both form and content.

(iv) Hiriyanna (1973:357-8) :—According to Hiriyanna also, the Advaitins believe that the Veda is *recreated* in each kalpa by Īśvara without any change either in its content or order. It is in this sense that it is authorless (apauruṣeya). While the Veda is eternal, it has different copies or issues in different kalpas and these copies are not eternal. He also holds that the only difference between Mīmāṃsā and Advaita in this respect is that the latter allows cyclic creation unlike the former (Hiriyanna 1973:358).

S 7.26 All this difference of opinion, I think, stems from a basic confusion between the Veda as a pramāṇa and the Veda as a pramā. In the present context the Veda is being considered as a form of testimony (śabda) and, therefore, as a pramāṇa. As thus conceived it is merely a set of words in a given order and a word (as a type as against token) exists either as an uttered sound or as a written sequence of symbols; and it ceases to be when it is neither uttered nor written. So when a cycle of creation comes to an end the set of words which constitutes the Veda also comes to an end; it comes again into being when a new cycle starts, so like most other things the Veda is non-eternal (but not momentary). There is, therefore, no basis for saying that the Veda *as a testimony* is eternal nor is there any basis for saying that it is apauruṣeya (authorless). When one is tempted as are Satprakasananda, Athalye and Hiriyanna to regard the Veda as eternal and authorless, what one has in mind is the content of the Veda; this content is the set of *truths* that the Vedic words or the sentences are said to express but these truths constitute pramā and not pramāṇa. Whether they are, in fact, eternal or not is irrelevant to the question at hand, namely, a consideration of the nature of scriptural testimony. Clearly Athalye, Satprakasananda and Hiriyanna fail to see this point.

S 7.27 It is to be noted that the text itself, namely, Vedānta-paribhāṣā (VP) clearly says that the Veda has an origin (*i.e.*, non-eternal) it comes into being in each cosmic projection and passes of being at the time of each cosmic dissolution.[20] The text also says, however, that 'apauruṣeya' refers to the content of an expression, not to its utterance nor to its authorship by a person implying thereby that the content (of the Vede) is eternal. This means that while the Veda as a pramāṇa is non-eternal the Veda as pramā is eternal. Thus the confussion between an expression and its content referred to above is also present in VP. to some extent : God *recreates* the Veda in exactly the same form in each kalpa (fn. 7.19).

S 7.28 It has been remarked above (S 7.24-7) that Advaitins seem to effect a compromise between the two opposite views of Nyāya and Mīmāṃsa on the question of pauruseyata or otherwise of the Veda. Indeed such a belief is shared by secondary authors like Athalye (1974:346), and S. Murthy (1974:49-50). But in the light of the confusion between the Veda as a pramāṇa and Veda as a pramā; and the much wider confusion between an expression and its content, the tenability of this belief needs to be examined. The essence of the alleged compromise of the Advaitins is that the Veda is non-eternal, produced anew by God in each kalpa; and yet it is apauruṣeya since even God has no freedom in *recreating* it. But if the Veda is to be taken in the sense of pramāṇa as it must be in this context, then surely there is no question of its being eternal. It is after all merely a set of sentences and like any other thing at all, is destroyed at the time of cosmic dissolution. The eternality of the Veda even in the sense of the pramāṇa would have been maintained if the Advaitins subscribe to the eternality of the varṇa and the Vedic order but they do not do. And even if they had done so, they could not have in that case subscribed to the non-eternality of the Veda at the same time, without self-contradiction. The apparent plausibility of the alleged compromise arises simply because of the confusion shown above; once the confusion is removed the question ceases to make sense.

Notes and References

1. śrutyanusāriṇyaḥ samṛtayaḥ pramāṇam . . . "The smṛtis agreeing with the Upaniṣads (śruti) are to be accepted as valid. . ." SBBS 2.1.1. Translated by Gambhirananda 1972:302. See MS 1.3.3.
2. When Athalye (1974:344-5) says whole of Vedic literature is divided into these four kinds, he employs expression Vedic literature in Bloomfeild's wider of the two senses (S 7.2).
3. āmānyasya kriyārthatvādānarthakyamatadarthānām tasmādanityamucyate. "The Veda being for the sacrifice, the portion which is not for the sacrifice is useless, therefore it cannot be said to be eternal." MS 1.2.1.
4. MS 1.1.24-31; Athalye 1974:345; Murty 1974:212; Radhakrishnan 1977b:392.
5. See for slight variation of this argument NM 214 on Mīmāṃsakas' view.
6. asya mahato bhūtasya niḥśvasitametaddadṛgvedo yajurvedaḥ sāmavedoatharvāngirasa. Bṛhadāraṇyaka-upaniṣad 2.4.10. NK 803; Athalye 1974:345.
7. varṇā nityāḥ 'sa evāyaṃ gakāra' iti pratyabhijñābalāt. "Letters are eternal (since this must be granted on the strength of the recognitive judgement, 'This (letter) 'ga' is the same as that (letter) 'ga.' " TD 62. Translated by C. Bhattacharya 1975:195. Hiriyanna 1973:310.
8. utpanno gakāro naṣṭo iti pratītyā varṇānāmanityatvāt. "For on account of the (common) experience that (the letter) 'ga' (which is only a sound) has originated and (the letter) 'ga' has ceased to be (it must be granted that) letters are not eternal." TD 62. Translated by C. Bhattacarya 1975:196. BP 167.
9. varṇarāśiḥ kramavyaktaḥ padamityabhidhīyate. varṇānāṃ cāvināśitvāt. . . "A word is a series of letters which manifest themselves in a close succession. But these letters are indestructible. . ." NM 188. J.V. Bhattacarya 1978:427. Hiriyanna 1973:310.
10. Śabda here does not mean tastimony which is a statement composed of words, there is thus an ambiguity in the word, 'śabda' : it means a pada or word and sometimes a testimony which is a statement. Still other times also means sound (dhvani). See TS 33.

11. tatra yathā dhūmāgnyornaisargika . . .sambāndhaḥ . . . śabdārthavosāmsi-ddhika. . . "In case of smoke and fire the relation. . .between smoke and fire is natural . . . Similarly the relation . . . holding between word and meaning is natural one." NM 221. Translated by J.V. Bhattacharya 1978:501.
12. In addition to all these difficulties to Mīmāṃsakas' naturalism, there is also the pervasive difficulty of what precisely the word 'artha' means. Sometimes it is taken as sence and some times as reference and hence, a frequent confusion between these two senses. The criticism of naturalism mentioned here applies respectively of whether 'artha' is taken as sense or reference.
13. vaidikan īśvaroktatvātsarvameva pramāṇam. "All Vedic sentences are instruments of valid knowledge, because they are uttered by god." TS 62. Translated by C. Bhattacharya 1975:195 TD 62: NM 213-20.
14. 'tasmāttepānātrayo Vedā ajāyanta' iti śruteśca. "Moreover, there is (in support of this view) the scriptural text. "From that meditating one (*i.e.*, from God), the three Vedas originated " TD 62. Translated by C. Bhattacharya 1975;195.
15. vedātkartravabodhe tu spaṣṭamanyonyasaṃśrayam. tato vedapramāṇatvaṃ vedātkartruśca niścayaḥ. Cited in NM 215. See J.V. Bhattacharya 1978:488.
16. paṭādirscarām dṛṣṭva tasya cetsā anumīyate. vede api racanāṃ dṛṣṭvā kartṛtvaṃ tasya gamyatām. "We infer the existence of a weaver who has made a cloth etc., from the object which has been created by him. Similarly, we infer the existence of the author of the Vedas from the arrangement of words contained in them (the Vedas)." NM 218. Translated by J.V. Bhattacharya 1978:495.
17. āsattiyogyatākānsātātparyajñāmīṣyate kāraṇam. "The knowledge of contignity, consistency expecancy and intention is the cause (of verbal comprehension)." BP 82-3. Translated by Madhavananda 1977:171.
18. itthaṃca vedasthaleapi tātparya jñānārthamīśvaraḥkalpyate. Thus even in the case of the Vedas, for the sake of the apprehension of the intention, the existence of God is assumed.'' Translated by Madhavenda 1977:171.
19. . . . sargādhyakāle parameśvaraḥ pūrvasargasiddhavedāpūrvīsamānānupūrvīkaṃ vedam viracitavān. ',. . . in the beginning of cosmic projection, the Lord produced Vedas having a sequence of words similar to that which had already existed in the Vedas in the previous cosmic projection. . .'' VP 114. Transiated by Madhavananda 1972:115 6 See SBBU 2.4.10.
20. varṇapadavākyasamudāyasya vedasya viyadādivat sṛṣṭikālīnotpattikatvaṃ pralayakālīnadhvaṃsapratiyogitvañca. "The Vedas, which are a collection of syllables words and sentences origieate like the ether etc., at the time of cosmic projection and are counterpositives of the destruction that takes place at the time of cosmic dissolution." VP 113. Translated by Madhvananda 1972;113-4.
21. na tu tadvijātīyaṃ yedamiti na sajātīypccāraṇāpekṣoceāraṇaviṣayatvaṃ pauruṣeyaivaṃ vedasya. "Hence the Vedas, not being the object of utterance that is independent of any utterance of the same kind, are not conneced with a person." VP 115. Translated by Madhavananda 1972:116.

8

INDEPENDENCE OF ŚABDA-PRĀMAṆA

S 8.1. There is a considerable discussion on this question in the traditional literature. The Vaiśeṣikas answer this question negatively and reduce testimony to inference.[1] C. Bhattacharya (1975 : 209-10) gives a clear account of the Vaiśeṣikas' reduction of testimony to inference. Suppose I learn from testimony that 'the daffodil is yellow', the Vaiśeṣika tries to show that this case of testimonial knowledge is just inferential knowledge and that it can be cast in the form of the syllogism as follows :

A 1. Thesis (pratijñā) : The sentence, 'the daffodil is yellow' has meaning

2. Reason (hetu) : because it possesses expectancy, competency, proximity and intention

3. Example (udāharaṇa) : Whatever sentence has expectancy, competency etc. has meaning, for example the sentence "Bring the pot."[2]

Gangeśa's criticism of this reduction is very revealing. He gives four reasons why such reduction will not do (Vidyabhusana 1971 : 446-7). The first and the most important of them is that the inference A does not involve knowledge of actual things but merely knowledge of recollected things. His second reason is but a consequence of the first : it is that the vyāpti in A does not hold. Viśvanātha is in full agreement with Gangeśa on this point (SM

140-1). Udayana also seems to have the same thing in mind though he expresses it in some what different words (Athalye 1974 : 348). Gangeśa's third reason also stems from the same consideration, namely, that activity proceeds from knowledge of actual things but not from the knowledge of their ideas. His fourth reason is independent : it is that introspective evidence (anuvyavasāya) shows that testimony is different from inference.

S 8.2. Jayanta Bhaṭṭa also criticises the attempts to reduce testimony to inference. But his criticism is directed to Buddhists rather than the Vaiśeṣikas. But this detail is immaterial since the Buddhist reduction in essence is the same as the Vaiśeṣika reduction. Jayanta Bhaṭṭa's criticism of Buddhist reduction is also in substance the same as the criticism of the Vaiśeṣika reduction by Udayana, Gangeśa, Viśvanātha, Annaṃbhaṭṭa, etc. It is that vyāpti employed in the reduction just does not hold.[3]

S 8.3. NBh (2.1.50-2) pays much attention to the reduction of testimony to inference without identifying the schools who make such reductions. Judging from NM (139-43) which is well known commentary on NS and NBh it would appear that the opponents whom Vātsyāyana has in mind are the Buddhists.[4] And the Vātsyāyana's reply to them is interesting, it is that the meaning of a word is conventional not natural, nor necessary.[5] How interesting this is will be clear presently (S 8.4).

S 8.4. Most of the discussion regarding whether or not testimony has an independent status as a pramāṇa is instructive and illuminating both for the error and the insight it brings to light. Both the Vaiśeṣika and Buddhist reduction of testimony to inference suffers from two important and related confusions. The first of these is the confusion between sense and reference ; and the second, the confusion between meaning and truth. When the Vaiśesikas (and the Buddhists) talk about meaning of individual words, they pass from sense to reference and as a consequence when they talk about sentence they pass from meaning to truth. The vyāpti in A on the face of it is illegitimate. The word 'meaning' (artha) there means sense or proposition. But the conclusion, derived, with the help of that vyāpti, employs 'artha' in the sense of truth. What the vyāpti along with the other premisses warrants as a conclusion is that the sentence in question is meaningful not that it is true. That meaning and truth are different hardly needs to be emphasised. Even false sentence can be meaningful just as even non-referring expressions can be meaningful.

The Naiyāyikas are in the right tract while criticising the reductionist attempt precisely because they are aware, at least in the context, of the distinction between sense and reference ; and meaning and truth. Their statement that in an inference A, there is really no vyāpti, amounts to saying that the vyāpti is false if meaning is taken as truth and that if meaning is taken as proposition or sense the intended conclusion, namely, the sentence in question is true, does not follow.

It was remarked above that Vātsyāyana's reply to reductionists, namely, the meaning of an expression is conventional, is interesting. It is so because it also reveals the same insight into the distinction between sense and reference, whether a sentence which is about the reference of its components is true has to be decided empirically and not deductively. On the other hand whether a sentence which is about the senses of its components is true can be decided apriori. Vātsyāyana's criticism amounts to saying that the reductionists pass from apriori claim to empirical claim and that in this they are simply wrong.

The Naiyāyikas also on independent considerations argue for the autonomy of testimony : they appeal to introspective evidence to establish the autonomy. But on this they are obviousiy on slippery grounds for it is equally open to the reductionists to claim that introspection (anuvyavasāya) supports identity claim.

The above defence of Naiyāyikas does not mean that their conclusion regarding the autonomy of testimony is right. It simply amounts to the claim that they are right in their refutation of the reductionists' reasons. The question, therefore, still remains whether testimony is an independent pramāṇa. And we have to answer this question on our own with the appropriate textual backing.

S 8.5. As noticed above the only plausible criterion of the independence of pramāṇa given in the traditional texts is the uniqueness of object (NBh 1.1.3 ; NM 33). This is emphasised not only by Vātsyāyana and Jayanta Bhaṭṭa but also by Śaṅkara

(SBBS 1.1.4) himself. This criterion means that for a pramāṇa to be considered independent there must be at least one object which is known by it alone and not by any other pramāna (S 5.4). This of course as was pointed out earlier (S 5.4) allows the possibility of convergence of pramāṅas, *i.e.*, one and the same object is known as, in fact is usually the case, by more than one pramāna. This is the one principal criterion and all others mentioned in the texts such as novelty, introspection etc., are untenable (SS 5.2-3).

Judging by the criterion of the uniqueness of object we can see without much difficulty that the scriptural testimony qualifies for autonomy : there are unique and supra sensible objects which, we are told, it alone can know.[6] Even Montague (1958 : 46, 56-7) who, in general, argues for the reducibility of testimony to sense or reason, *i.e.*, perception or inference recognises this point. He maintains that inspite of its general reducibility testimony is still recognised as a source of knowledge because, at least in some cases, it gives knowledge which cannot be given by any other source (Montague 1958 : 56-7). This position of Montague amounts to saying that testimony of certain kind (*i.e.*, alaukika or scriptural testimony) is autonomous because it satisfies the criterion of uniqueness of object. Montague himself does not of course explicitly talk of uniqueness of object, but what he explicitly does amounts to the recognition of the autonomy of scriptural testimony on the ground of its conformity to the uniqueness of object.

S 8.6. As for ordinary or laukika testimony it is obvious that it can be reduced either to perception or inference. Instead of accepting the words of a laukika āpta it is theoretically open to me to obtain direct knowledge for myself. It is only because of limitation of space and time and of other contingency of personal circumstances that instead of trying to obtain the knowledge by myself I take resourse to the words of a laukika āpta. This is recognised by Montague (1958:39-45) and Hospers (1971:135-6). And this also ties in with what I have said about the justification condition of testimonial knowledge (S 3.4).

S 8.7 There are, however, persons like Datta (1927:354-78, 1963:201-11; 1972:336-8) who question the reducibility of even ordinary testimony to perception or inference. Refferring to Montague's argument that ordinary testimony can be conflicting and that in such case conflict can be resolved by an appeal to sense or reason (*i.e.*, perception or inference). Datta (1927:357; 1963:208; 1972:348) maintains that conflicting testimonies need not come in the way of automony of testimony as a source of knowledge just as a conflict of perceptions can be resolved by further perceptions so also conflict of testimonies may be overcome by further testimonies. Datta fails to see that while the resolution of conflicts in the two cases may be parallel, the parallalism does not extend to the autonomy of the two sources of knowledge, it leaves unaffected the question of the automony of the two sources. Datta adduces three considerations for the automony of testimony. The first of these is that just because words of an āpta are seen or heard (*i.e.*, perceived) it does not follow that testimony is reducible to perception (Datta 1927:356; 1963:206). This is of course triviality, but it is unfair to suggest as Datta seems to be doing that autonomy of testimony is based on this triviality. The second of Datta's reasons for the autonomy of laukika śabda is that even perception sometimes is validated by testimony (1972:338). But this is no ground for saying that perception is reducible to testimony. Similarly, just because testimony is validated by perception, it does not follow, Datta (1972:328) seems to argue, that testimony is reducible to perception. Here again his argument is unacceptable because testimony may validated perception only on some occasions but testimony (*i.e*.. of laukika variety) *always* and *in principle* is validated by perception or inference, and this fact makes it reducible to the latter. The third reason that Datta adduces in support of the automony of even ordinary testimony is that at least some perception of past events is not repeatable and that, therefore, at least the testimony concerning such events is not reducible to either perception or inference. Quine and Ullian (1970:18) also maintain :

> . . . testimony is often essential and irreducible because of unrepeatable observations.

S 8.8 This is indeed a weightly consideration in support of the autonomy of ordinary testimony but is it conclusive ? Even though observations of past events may not be strictly speaking repeatable (*i.e.*, in so far as such events are taken as tokens, there is still a sense in which events are repeatable in the sense of type) and hence their observations are also repeatable and the possibility of reducing testimony to inference is wide open. However, one might suggest that there may be certain rare and unique events which are not all repeatable, not even in the sense of type, and it is in such cases the testimony remains fundamental and autonomous. This last consideration, if true, would conclusively establish autonomy of even mundane testimony but is it true ? I do not think so for even if there are events which are absolutely unique and unrepeatable it still does not mean mundane testimony is autonomous for I could still say that testimony about such events could be reduced to potential or possible perceptual statements, the direct knowledge that the āpta had in the past, I also could have had, were I also placed in the same or similar circumstances, I could myself have observed the events if I were then alive and at the time and place of the event's occurrence with sufficient motivation to observe it. After all we know that physical object statements can be plausibly reduced to statements about actual or possible sensations (compare Mill's statement that a physical object is the permanent possibility of sensation). Why should a similar project not be plausible in the case of mundane testimony ? In actual fact the latter project is not only plausible but also quite convincing.

To conclude then while autonomy may be conceded to alaukika śabda it cannot be conceded to laukika śabda and this conclusion, I think, is in harmony with the spirit of the texts themselves.

Notes and References

1. The Vaiśeṣikas are not alone in reducing testimony to inference even the Prābhākaras of the Pūrvamīmāṃsa school do so, but only partially, that is, while the Vaiśeṣikas reduce testimony as a whole to inference, the Prābhākaras reduce only the laukika or pauruṣeya variety of it to inference considering autonomy to the alaukika or apauruseya variety of testimony. See MN 106-8.
   It may be noted that while in the case of the Naiyāyikas the two distinctions alaukika and laukika, pauruṣeya and apauruṣeya do not coincide; in the case Pūrva-mīmāṃsa and Advaita-vedāna they do. For the Naiyāyikas both the laukika and alaukika testimony are pauruṣeya (S 6.3).
   The Buddhists also reduce testimony to inference but partially (NM 316-8). See for detals Vidyabhusana 1971:287-8; Radhakrishnan 1977b:6-111,
2. nanvetāni padāni svasmāritārthasaṃsargavanti ākānkśādimatpadakadambakatvāt madvākyavadityanumānādeva saṃsargajñānasaṃbhavāchchabdo na pramānantaramiti cenna. "Words are not an additional instrument of valid knowledge, since the knowledge of the connection (of the meanings

of the different words or a group or them) can be had from just an inference (like) : These words refer to the connection of the meanings which are recalled by them, because they form a collection of words which possess expectancy etc., just as my sentence (such as 'Bring the pot')." TD 63. Translated by Bhattacharya 1975:197.

tathāhi—damdena gāmanayetyadilaukikapadāni yajetetyadivaidikapadāni vā tātparyaviṣayasmāritapadārthasamsargapramā pūrvakāṇi—ākānkṣādimatpadakadambatvāt, ghaṭamānayeti pada kadambavāt. yadvā etepadārthā mithaḥ samsargavamtaḥ-yogya-tādimatpadopasthāpitatvāt, tādṛaśaśabdārthavāt. "For example, secular words like, 'Drive the cow in with a stick', or Vedic words like, '(One) should perform sacrifices', are preceded by a valid knowledge of that connection among the recalled meanings of words, which is the subject-matter of the speaker's intention, because they are group of words possessing expectancy etc. analogous to a group of words like. 'Bring the jar.' Or these meanings of words are connected with one another, because they are recalled by words possessing consistency etc., analogously to words of that kind." SM 140-1. Translated by Madhavananda 1977:232. See Vidyabhusana 1971:446; *Sapta-padārthi* 155.

See for further details 'Śabda-Śakti-prakāśikā' in Vidyabhusana 1971-470-2.

3. tatra vākyamānavagatasambandhameva vākyārthamavagamayitumalam. "But a sentence reveals its meaning without depending upon the knowledge of the relation between a sentence and its meaning." NM 143. Translated by J.V. Bhattacharya 1978:318.

4. . . .evam mitena śabdena paścānmīyatearthoanupalabhyamāna ityanumānam śabdaḥ. ". . .and in the case of word, also an object which is not already known (by means of perception) comes to be cognised afterwards by means of the already known word—such is the process of verbal cognition. Thus we find that 'word' is only inference." NBh 2.1.50. Translated by Jha 1939:177.

sambandhayośca śabdārthayoḥ sambandhaprasidvau śabdopalabdherarthagrahaṇam, yathā sambandvayorlingalinginoh sambandhapratītau lingopalabdhau lingigrahaṇamiti. "As a matter of fact, we find that the cognition of a thing by means of a word appears only when there is a relationship between the word and the thing denoted by it, and this relationship is fully known; exactly in the same manner as the cognition of the probandum by means of the inferential probans appears only when there is a relationship between the probans and the probandum, and this relationship is fully known." NBh 2.1.52. Translated by Jha 1939:178.

5. na sambandhakāritam śabdārthavyavasthāṇam. . . samayakāritam. NBh 2.1.56.

6. NBh 1.1.3; NM 33; SBBS 1.1.4.

9

VAIDIKA ŚABDA, REVELATION AND REASON

S 9.1 Despite their differences regarding details concerning the nature of scriptural testimony the fact remains that all the three schools, Nyāya, Mīmāṃsā and Advaita-vedānta identify scriptural testimony with the Veda. They might emphasise different portions of the Veda in keeping with their general outlook (S 7.4). According to all the three schools scriptural testimony gives knowledge of unique sort-knowledge generally not obtainable, at least in its distinctive part, from other pramāṇas. It is generally concerned with supra-sensible entities. That such knowledge is genuine knowledge; that in other words, it satisfies all the conditions of knowledge has already been seen (S 3.5). That scriptural testimony is an independent form of testimony has also been seen (SS 8.1-8). There yet remained some questions regarding this form of testimony which deserve our attention. One such question is : how is revelation related to reason; but before answering this question it is desirable to consider the nature of revelation, for at least two reasons : (i) reason is normally contrasted with the revelation; (ii) the Veda as emerged from the foregoing discussion is said to be revealed to certain selected persons by God according to certain Indian schools such as Advaita-vedānta. What then is revelation ?

S 9.2 According to Hick (1979:52) "revelation may be defined as the communication of some truth by God to a rational creature through means which are beyond the ordinary course of nature." A similar definition is given by Alston (1963:389). Such a definition would indicate that revelation is a process in which God is an active agent and man is a passive recipient. The result of such a process is of couse what is revealed; such a result is often confused with the process, for example, even noted authors like S. Murty (1974:9-10), Hiriyanna (1972:180-1) and Satprakasanda (1974:256) actually identify revelation with the śruti (the Veda). What we are here concerned is with the process and not with the result of its process. The revelation as thus defined is said to be propositional because it is a revelation of truths. In this type of revelation God chooses a certain person for reasons of his cwn even if such a person is not intellectually confident nor morally superior. God elevates him intellectually and morally to a level where he in a position to apprehend the truths revealed to him and is able to communicate them adequately to others. But this is not the only type of revelation; there is also what is called a non-propositional revelation (Hick 1979:59-60). In this latter type it is not some truth that is revealed but God himself or some event at God's instance. Even in the second type the basis of selecting a recipient is the same *i.e.*, recipient is chosen on God's reasons thus there is an element of grace involved in both kinds of revelation.

S 9.3 In the context of scriptural testimony what is relevant is propositional variety of revelation and not so much of the non-propositional variety. In thc discussion of this type of revelation, there is often a discussion in the Indian writings of the so-called criteria of revelation, for example, Vacaspati Misra[1] in his Bhāmati mentions six criteria. Hiriyanna (1973:180-1) on the other hand, mentions on the basis of MS 1.1.5 only three of the six marks as determining the revealed truths, namely, consistency, novelty and intelligibility. Jayanta Bhaṭṭa lays down still other conditions of revealed truths (scriptures), namely, celebrity, popularity, universality, objectivity, and credibility.[2]

Even cursory examination of these various criteria (conditions, marks, characteristics etc.), show that they are clearly inadequate as criteria. Even non-revealed truth can satisfy them. Apart from this deficiency there is also a further and more serious deficiency in them, namely, that they just cannot be criteria of revelation as a process, at best they can be considered as criteria of revelation in the sense of the product, and so considered they are as just remarked obviously deficient. Their discussion in the context of scriptural testimony is a further evidence of the very pervasive confusion between the revelation as the process and revelation as product.

S 9.4 The traditional discussion of revelation in Indian writings reveal another confusion between revelation and intuition, for example, Matilal (1971:166), says : "There is the belief in the possibility of a kind of knowledge which we may call revelation, intuition, even direct confrontation with reality." Rorty (1967:204) defines intuition as 'immediate apprehension which covers both sensuous and supra-sensuous apprehensions.' Two broad types of intuitions are distinguished, namely, empirical (including mathematical) and mystical (Hospers 1971.136-9) and both these types are covered by above definition. In the context of scriptural testimony empirical intuition is obviously beside the point. What is involved in this context is mystical intuition. Montague (1958: 54-5) defines mystical intuition as : "that it is that capacity of the soul by which man comes into direct telepathic communication with disembodied spirits, with mysterious cosmic energies or even with God himself." In other words, mystical intuition is the transcendent faculty by which man apprehends the suprasensible and supra-rational in direct and immediate manner.[3] Thus, strictly speaking intuition is faculty or process but like revelation it is often confused with the result or content of the process of intuition, in other words, with what is intuited. Taken as a faculty or a process, intuition shows that man is active in it, man as against the object of intuition be it God or other supra-sensible entities. In revelation on the other hard, man is a passive recipient while the active role belongs to God as explained above (S 9.2). Intuition is a human faculty but revelation can never be considered such; thus intuition and revelation need to be clearly distinguished and the observance of this distinction helps us in understanding several traditional points better.

S 9.5 If revelation is understood in the above sense, the Veda in the sense of scriptural testimony cannot be revealed for the simple reason that is is not a truth (pramā); but scriptural testimony is a pramāṇa, and not pramā and what is revealed cannot be a pramāṇa. The traditional Indian thinkers are prompted to talk of the Veda as revealed because they confuse the revelation as a process with its content.

Again if revelation is understood in proper sense as indicated above, how is it related to reason ? In other words, if both revelation and reason are understood as processes, how are they related ? The question regarding the relationship between reason and revelation is explicitly and prominently discussed in the Advaita-vedānta school even though attention to it is not entirely lacking in Nyāya and Mīmāṃsā.

S 9.6 Let me, therefore, proceed to consider the Advaita answer to this question. The role of reason is highlighted in a surprisingly large number of cases in Advaita-vedānta. Śaṅkara, for instance, declares that even if hundred scriptures say that fire is cold or the sun does not give heat or light, they are not to be believed (fn 0.1). Again he says in Māṇḍūkya-kārikā-bhāṣya[4] that the nature of Brahman is known by reason. Devaraja (1972:59-60) claims that according to Śaṅkara Brahman is known by reason alone.[5] There is also frequent emphasis on manana or critical reflection,[6] for understanding śruti. Reason is also said to help in clarifying and determining the purport of śruti (Mahadevan 1976: 57). Such statements as these give the impresssion that the Advaitins are rationalists per excellence. This impression is, however, in the ultimate analysis, not true for the statements just referred to are invariably hedged in by certain very serious qualifications which severely limit the role of reason, for example, Śaṅkara's statement that even if hundred scriptures say that a thing that goes against our perceptual experiences, they are to be disbelieved is qualfied by saying revelation has no place in the realm of ordinary experience and reason. But in it our proper realm of revelation reigns supreme. Further, Śaṅkara's statement in the Kathabhāṣya (fn 9.5) says that Brahman is known by reason is contrasted by another statement of Śaṅkara's in the Kathabhāṣya[7] that Brahman cannot be known by reason or tarka. Devaraja (1972:64) virtually neutralistes his above statement with the qualification that only that reason which is backed by scriptural testimony can know Brahman.[8] Again the above statements which assign to reason the functions of clarification and determination of the purport of the śruti give it a subordinate position in relation to what is revealed. The limits are laid down by scriptural testimony and the activity of clarification must go on within the limits, reason thus has no autonomy, only revelation has.

S 9.7 The Advaita school's overall position concerning the relationship between reason and revelation is that revelation in its legitimate realm, namely, śruti, is supreme and reason can only play secondary role to it *i.e.*, revealed truths provide the subject matter for reason, reason cannot question what is revealed but can only elucidate and enlarge and expound it. Hume said that reason is the slave of passion with appology, we can say for the Advaitins reason is not to be the slave of what is revealed. Only that reason which is reinforced by revelation can play any role in the context of apprehending Vedic truths. Reason in this context does not mean just rational faculty but also includes the ordinary senses.

S 9.8 Thus the first impression that the Advaitins are rationalists par excellence virtually disappears because of the increasingly heavy qualifications added by the Advaitins. Hiriyanna (1973:182) puts the situation very succinctly. According to the Advaitins, the rationalists' position is : "They do not know because they reason; rather they reason because they know."

S 9.9 The Nyāya position regarding the relationship between reason and revelation is similar to that of Advaita-vedānta. Gautama (NS 2.1.60) says that reason can only try to make sense what is revealed but it can never question it for instance even when there is a clear contradiction between two Vedic statements :[9] "The oblation should be offered after sunrise," and "The oblation should be offered before sunrise." Reason is supposed to resolve the contradiction by saying that the worshipper should make his own choice either morning or evening and follow it consistently—a strange reconcilisation indeed. This position of Gautam is repeated by Vātsyāyana in NBh (2.1.60) and Jayanta Bhaṭṭa in NM (249, 251). Athalye (1974:290-91) commenting on TD 49 holds that according to the Nyāya school reason can only clarify and elucidate what is already revealed. C. Bhattacharya (1975:114) also thinks that according to Nyāya reason can only corroborate what is revealed but can never question or contradict it. The position of Mīmāṃsaka on this issue is not far different, reason, must see that revelation is consistent and intelligible but it can never alter or amend it. In other words, reason can only supplement and never supplant revelation (Hiriyanna 1973:181,298).

Notes and References

1. upakramo upasaṁhārāv abhyāso, apūrvata phalam arthavado upapatti ca liṇgaṁ tātparya nirṇaye. "The marks determinative of purport are: the harmony of the initial and concluding passages (upakrama-upasaṁhāra),

repetition (abhyāsa), novelty (apūrvata), fruitfulness (phala), glorification by eulogistic passages or condemnation by deprecatory passages (arthavāda) and intelligibility in the light of reasoning (upapatti)." Cited in Mahadevan 1976:57.

2. mahājanasamūhe ye prasiddhiṁ prāpurāgamāḥ. kṛtaśca bahūbhiryeṣāṁ śiṣṭairiha parigṛḥ: adhya pravartamānāśca napūrvā iva bhānti ye. yeṣāṁ na mūlaṁ lobhādi yebhyo nodvijate jahaḥ. tepameva pramāṇatvamāgamānāmiheṣyate. The āgamas (*scriptures*) are held to be authentic if they satisfy the following conditions (1) they must attain celebrity among the circle of the great persons; (2) They must be accepted by a large number of men of good conduct; (3) Though they may have been recently composed yet they should not instruct such conduct as appears to be unprecedented; (4) The greed of money should not be motive of their composition; (5) They should not preach such doctrines as cause anxity to others. NM 248, Translated by Bhattacharya 1978:562.

3. Mysticism is the philosophical theory which centeres around intuition in fact Montague (1958:54) defines myticism as "... theory that truth can be attained by a super-rational and super-sensuous faculty of intuition is mysticism."

4. advaitaṁ kimāgamamātreṇa pratipattavyam āhosvitarkeṇāpītyata āha. Śakyate tarkeṇāpi jñātum. "Now it is asked whether non-duality can be established only by scriptural evidence or whether it is proved by reasoning as well. It is said in reply that it is possible to establish non-duality by reasoning as well." SBMU 3.1. Translated by Nikhilananda 1974:133.

5. buddhirhi naḥ pramāṇam sadasatoryāthātmyāvagame. "And reason, indeed, is the proof for us in ascertaining the real nature of the existent and the non-existent." SBKU 6.12. Translated by Gambhirananda 1977:210.

6. ... śravaṇamanananididhyāsanānyapi jñānasādhanāni "... hearing, reflection and meditation also are means to knowledge." VP 212. Translated by Madhavananda 1972:213.

7. atoananyaprokta ātmanyutpannā yeyamāgamapratipādhyātmamatiḥ naiṣā tarkeṇa svabuddhyābhyūhamātreṇa āpaneyā na prāpaṇīyetyarthaḥ. "Therefore *eṣā*, this wisdom about the self, as presented by the Vedas, that arises when the self is taught by one who has besome identified with It; *tarkeṇa* through argumentation—called up merely by one's own intellect; *na āpaneya*, is not to be attained." SBKU 2.9. Translated by Gambhirananda 1977:134.

8. ... śrutyanugrhīta eva hyātra tarkoanubhavavāṅgatvenāśrīyate.... for logic, conforming to the upaniṣads, is alone resorted to here as a subsidiary means helping realization." SBBS 2.1.6. Translated by Gambhirananda 1972:314.

9. tadaprāmāṇyamanratavyāghātapunaruktadoṣebhyaḥ. "That (word) cannot be regarded as an instrument of right cognition, because of such defects as (A) Falsity (B) Contradiction, and (C) Tautology." (Pūrva Pakṣa) NS 2.1.58. Translated by Jha 1939:184

(B) havane—'udite hotavyam anudite hotavyam samayādyuṣite hotavyam' iti—vidhāya. "For instance, in regard to the (agnihotra) oblation, we find such injunctions as—(a) 'The oblation should be offered after sunrise,' (b) The oblation should be offered before sunrise.' NBh 2.1.58. Translated by Jha 1939:185. abhyupetya kalabhede doṣavacanat. "The deprecatory assertion applies to the changing of particular time after having (once) adopted it." NS 2.1.60. Translated by Jha 1939:187.

10

VAIDIKA ŚABDA AND CRITERIA OF TRUTH (I)

S 10.1 Besides the question of relationship between reason and revelation another question with which the subject of scriptural testimony is connected is that of what is customarily known as validity. This is strictly the question of truth than validity for, the concept of validity in the contemporary logical jargon is normally applied to arguments while the concept of truth is applied to statements or propositions. But how is the question of truth related to the subject of scriptural testimony ? The answer is that the traditional theories of truth are related to the question whether the Veda (scriptural testimony) is authored or authorless. NM declares that svataḥ-pramāṇyatva of the Veda is a consequence of the apauṣrueyatva or eternality of the Veda for any defect is due to the authoring agency, and authorlessness is a guarantee that it is free from all defects and hence of its intrinsic validity.[1] And to this, Matilal (1968b:322-2) adds that the theory of intrinsic validity of the Veda was later developed into the general theory of self-validity of any cognition *i.e.*, svataḥ-pramāṇya-vāda in general. Hence one can say that svataḥ-pramāṇya-vāda, one of the two main traditional theories of truth, is related to the question of whether or not the Veda is authored.

S 10.2 Similarly, the other main traditional theory of truth, namely, parataḥ-paramāṇya-vāda also shows a relationship between the question of truth and the authorship of the Veda (scriptural testimony). According to that theory the Veda is authored by

God, and God being omniscient cannot author what is defective or false. Therefore, the Vedic statements are necessarily true.[2] But their truth is known not intrinsically but extrinsically.[3] And the fact that they are authored by God is enough gurantee of such correspondence. Hence the scriptural testimony is related even on parataḥ-pramāṇya-vāda to the question of truth. It is thus seen that the two important traditional theories of truth, namely, svataḥ-pramāṇya-vāda and parataḥ-pramāṇya-vāda are very much relevant in elucidating the concept of scriptural testimony. Apart from their bearing on scriptural testimony these two traditional theories are by themselves of philosophical interest. The nature and criteria of truth constitute an important topic in contempory epistemology and it is interesting to note that the traditional Indian thinkers made significant contribution on this subject. A treatment, therefore, of traditional Indian theories of truth is doubly relevant and desirable. I shall, therefore, proceed to the consideration of them. Before doing so one important point concerning these two traditional theories of truth needs to be emphasised. These are theories concerning our knowledge of truth. In other words, they are theories of criteria of truth, not of the nature of truth. In this they simply contrast with the contemporary western theories of truth which are primarily concerned with the nature of truth and only secondarily with the criteria of truth. This is illustrated by the three classical western theories of truth, namely, the correspondence theory of truth, the coherence theory of truth and the pragmatic theory of truth. It is, therefore, somewhat misleading to describe svataḥ-pramāṇyavāda and parataḥ-pramāṇya-vāda as theories of validity of knowlepge as has been customarily done by secondary authors (Randle 1976:50; Hiriyanna 1973:261). They are really theories of tests of truth and both agree regarding the nafure of truth for both of them a true cognition is tadvati tatprakārako anubhavaḥ sa eva pramā (A cognition which has, for its subject, something which possesses the character which it (*i.e.*, the cognition) has for its predicate, is a valid cognition (TS 35; Vp 143). It should be clear from this that it would be very wrong to regard svataḥ-prāmāṇya-vāda as the self-evidence theory (Banerjee 1974.108-9) or the coherence theory of truth and paratah-prāmāṇya-vāda as the correspondence theory of truth as has been sometimes done (Chatterjee 1939:113).

S 10.3 Another important point that needs to be considered in the context of svataḥ-prāmāṇya-vāda and parataḥ-prāmāṇya-vāda is that they are only theories of criteria of truth not necessarily of falsity. It is strange but true that in the Indian tradition the criteria of truth and of falsity do not coincide: while it is only in the case of Naiyāyikas and Sāṃkhyas there is a common theory for both truth and falsity. While the Naiyāyikas are paratastva-vādin regarding our apprehension of truth as well as falsity. The Sāṃkhyas are svatastva-vādin[4] regarding both truth values. But both Advaita-vedāntins and Mīmāṃsakas while being svataḥ-pramāṇya-vādins are parataḥ-apramāṇya-vādins. Similarly, Buddhists while being parataḥ-pramāṇya-vādins are svataḥ-apramāṇya-vādins. There are thus different permutations and combinations of svataḥ-prāmāṇya-vāda and parataḥ-prāmāṇya-vāda regarding truth and svataḥ-aprāmāṇya-vāda and parataḥ-aprāmāṇya-vāda regarding falsity. In this thesis, I have restricted myself to the traditional views of criteria of truth (not of falsity). In other words, I shall consider only that aspect of svataḥ-prāmāṇya-vāda and parataḥ-prāmāṇya-vāda which is concerned with our knowledge of truth and leave out that portion which deals with our knowledge of falsehood, even though two portions may be dealt with under the same theory by a particular school. It may be further noted that the designations svataḥ-prāmāṇya-vāda and parataḥ-prāmāṇya-vāda are given as a view of a particular school for knowledge of truth irrespective of its view on their knowledge of falsehood, for example, as remarked above, Advaitins and Mīmāṁsakas are called svataḥ-prāmāṇya-vādins even though they are parataḥ-aprāmāṇya-vādins.

S 10.4 *A theory of intrinsic truth (svataḥ-prāmāṇya-vāda)* :— Roughly speaking this is a theory that the truth of a statement is intrinsic to that statement and a true statement certifies its own truth. The theory immediately reminds us of today's thesis regarding apriori statements (that it is true independently of what happens in the world), and of analytic statements (that a statement is analytic if and only if its truth (or falsity) depends solely on the meanings of the terms it contains) but it must be emphasised that svataḥ-prāmāṇya-vāda is not merely a theory of apriori or analytic statements but a theory concerning the truth of any statement including what we call the empirical statements. That this is so can be seen from what its traditional advocates have to say regarding it.

S 10.5 In their discussion of truth traditional Indian thinkers distinguish between three different notions, namely, origin (utpatti), ascertainment (jñapti) and illumination or (prakāśatā) of a cognition. Origin (utpatti) is concerned with the question, 'what are the conditions that give rise to a cognition.' Ascertainment (jñapti) is concerned with the question, 'how does one know that a given cognition is true.' And finally illumination, or (prakāśatā) is concerned with the question, 'how is one aware of a cognition.' There are different theories concerning each one of these three notions and some of these cut across the two theories of truth, namely, svataḥ-prāmāṇya-vāda and parataḥ-prāmāṇya-vāda.[5] The really important question for us is one concerning the ascertainment (jñapti) for it alone is of epistemological significance, the other two are roughly psychological in character and their discussion is mostly scholastic as we shall presently see.

S 10.6 The traditional theory of intrinsic truth (svataḥ-prāmāṇya-vāda) also centers around the concepts of utpatti), jñapti and prakāśatā. It is desirable to set forth the views of svataḥ-prāmāṇya-vādins on these three topics briefly.

S 10.7 Origin (utpatti) : A true cognition according to svataḥ-prāmāṇya-vādins asises due to normal conditions and not due to any special condition or quality (guṇa)[6] as Naiyāyikas hold, for example, in the case of a true perceptual statement the normal conditions are good eyesight, sufficient light etc. and in the case of inferential statement normal conditions include liṅga-parāmarśa or vyāpti-viśiṣṭa-pakṣa-dharmatā-jñānaṃ. (The knowledge that a concomitant of the probandum is a character of the subject).[7] Strictly speaking the socalled normal conditions really include what parataḥ-prāmāṇya-vādins call the special quality (guṇa).[8] Thus the difference between svataḥ-prāmāṇya-vādins and parataḥ-prāmāṇya vādins with respect to the origin of a true cognition (utpatti) is merely verbal.

S 10.8 Illuminatton or manifestation (Prakāśatā) : As noted above prakāśatā is concerned with the question how do I know that I know; thus formulated it would appear that prakāśatā is concerned only with true cognitions for as we have seen before (S 1.3), knowledge is among other things a true cognition. However, there are authors like Mohanty (1966:4) who seem to think that prakāśatā is concerned with any cognition true or false. This is indicated for instance when Mohanty (1966:4) says : "The theory of prakāśa is in fact logically prior to the theory of prāmāṇya. . . .The theory of prakāśa is also wider in scope in as much as it pertains to all states of consciousness and not merely to knowledge." Even if prakāśatā is concerned with any cognition in the context of svataḥ-prāmāṇya-vāda, it gets limited to true cognitions only.[9]

S 10.9 Even amongst svataḥ-prāmāṇya-vādins there are two views regarding prakāśata of a cognition, namely, svataḥ-prakāśa-vāda (theory of self-manifestation) and paraiaḥ-prakāśa-vāda (theory of extrinsic manifestation). According to svataḥ-prakāśa-vāda a cognition manifests itself, in other words, when I know that p (where p is any proposition), I simultaneously also know that I know that p. Thus 'I know that p', and 'I know that I know that p' coincide (Matilal 1968a:125). According to parataḥ-prakāśa-vāda on the other hand, we are aware of a cognition through author cognition. This other cognition may be a case of introspection (anuvyavasāya) as held by Murāri Miśra or a case of inference as it is maintained by the Bhāṭṭas.[10]

S 10.10 The question of prakāśata is primarily psychological. It is better reformulated as "when we are aware of some things are we also aware of that awareness at the same time ?" The answer of svataḥ-prakāśa-vādins is that we are needed aware of awareness simultaneously; while that of prataḥ prakāśa-vādins is that our awareness of awareness is an after effect being due either to introspection or to inference (S 10.9).

S 10.11 The question of the origin of a cognition is psychological as suggested above (S 10.5) and like the question of prakāśatā is of little philosophical and epistemological significance. It is a matter of historical accident that these questions are mixed up with genuinely epistemological questions of the criteria of knowledge of truth. This latter question is dealt udder ascertainment (jñapti), though it is difficult to keep the three notions separate in reconstructing the traditional views on it.

S 10.12 Ascertainment (jñapti) : As remarked above jñapti is concerned with the question of criteria of knowledge of truth. The jñapti vāda of svataḥ-prāmāṇya-vāda, according to Advaitins and Prabhākaras' version, has two parts,[11] namely, svataḥ-siddha and svataḥ-prakāśatā (Satprakasananda 1974:112). A cognition is said to be svataḥ-siddha if the very normal conditions which give rise to a (true) cognition also give rise to its truth. In other words, truth of a cognition stems from the casual conditions of that cognition. To know the truth, therefore, we do not have to go beyond the conditions of its origin. Svataḥ-prakāśata-vāda states that the truth of every cognition stems from its own self-luminosity. In other words, a cognition in revealing itself also reveals its truth.[12] This would mean that the self-Validity of a cognition according to Advaitins and Prābhākaras follows from its self-luminosity and this would go counter to what I have said above (S 10.8), namely, that svataḥ-prakāśa-vāda is a theory which is applicably to any cognition in general true or false, and is not limited to true cognitions (Mohanty 1966:4). But this discrepancy is not without any textual basis (Mohanty 1966:6,8,11). J.N. Mohanty also in actual practice limits svataḥ-prakāsh-vāda to true cognitions even though he initially maintains that svataḥ prakāśa-vāda is a theory of any cognition true or false.

S 10.13 What does emerge from this exposition of jñapti vāda of svataḥ-prāmāṇya-vādins regarding their criterion of truth ? In other words what is the criterion of knowledge of truth according to svataḥ-prāmāṇya-vādins ? This question is not explicitly answered by traditional Indian thinkers but their answer is implicit in what they explicitly say. For example, the statement that a cognition in revealing itself also reveals its truth value, means in effect that there is really no criterion of truth. If a cognition reveals itself and attests its own truth, we need no aid or test for knowing truth of that cognition. But it is possible to ask whether the criterion is the totality of normal conditions which produces a true cognition. If the answer to this question is in the affirmative then the criterion could be formulated in the following fashion : "A cognition is true if and only if, the conditions that produce it are normal." But how is one to decide whether the conditions are normal ? It is difficult to see how there could be a test for normality independently of truth. Hence even if normality is construsted as the svataḥ-prāmāṇya-vādins' criterion it would beg the very question at issue and, therefore, it would be totally pointless. This account of jñapti-vāda of svataḥ-prāmāṇya-vādins confirms the difficulty noted above (S 10.11), namely, of keeping apart the three notions: utpatti, jñapti and prakāśatā, and in the above exposition of the traditional view of jñapti of svataḥ-prāmāṇya-vādins the concepts of prakāśatā and utpatti have inevitably crept in. But of course we can ignore these concepts and confine ourselves to the epistemological import of jñapti. This import according to svataḥ-prāmāṇya-vādins is just that there is no criterion, of truth since truth reveals itself. In this connection, two things must be noted : (i) svatah-prāmāṇya-vādins like Advaitins hold that knowledge (pramā) is conducive to fruitful activity;[13] (ii) they also hold that knowledge is that which is characterised by novelty and which is uncontradicted.[14] As for the question of novelty in (ii) it has been already pointed out (S 2.6) that it is not a necessary condition of knowledge. The same considerations would show that it is not even inseparable, though not a necessary condition of knowledge. In other words it cannot serve as criterion of truth. As for the non-contradictoriness (abādhitatva) in (ii), it is not difficult to see that this expression is used in paraphrasing the definition of truth as 'tadvati tatprakārakatvam (Vp 143) and Advaitins' intention is not to suggest even remotely that it would be criterion of truth. Even though reference is made to fruitful activity in (i) such reference in no way suggests that fruitful activity is intended as a criterion of truth. What is meant is that fruitful activity is a consequence of our knowledge of truth and not a criterion of truth: knowledge leads to fruitful activity because it is true; one does not know that a cognition is true on the ground that it leads to fruitful results. So the conclusion is inescapable that for svatah-prāmāṇya-vādins really there is no criterion of truth because none is needed. The svatah-prāmāṇya-vādins support their position of svatah-prāmāṇya-vāda by both positive and negative considerations. The notable among these are the following :

S 10.14 (i) A cognition is momentary in character and unless its truth is apprehended at the same time at which it arises its (truth) can never be apprehended in particular. In other words, the attempt to approach the truth of a cognition ab-extra is self-defeating for by the time a reference is made to an external condition the cognition in question ,could have ceased and its truth would have become forever inaccessible. The momentary character allows no scope for any external test and necessitates the theory of self-validity.[15]

S 10.15 This is of course the Mīmāṃsakas argument and so far as it goes it is not only plausible but also conclusive. Advaitins, however, do not accept the momentary character of the cognition and it is not clear what substitute argument they give in support of svataḥ-prāmāṇya-vāda. In fact, I have not come across any other positive argument in support of svataḥ-prāmāṇya-vāda whether from Advaitins or from Mīmāṃsakas (including Bhaṭṭas and Prābhākaras); or even from Sāṃkhyas. The above view of argument of Mīmāsaka is positive in character. However, there are at least three negative arguments in support of svataḥ prāmāṇya-vāda; all of them seem to establish svataḥ-prāmāṇya-vāda indirectly by refuting paratah-prāmāṇya-vāda. In particular, they try, to establish the thesis that a true cognition is self-revealing and that there is no need of criterion for knowing it by showing that the criterion that the rivals (parataḥ-prāmāṇya-vādins) propose is unacceptable.

S 10.16 (i) The test of fruitful activity adopted by parataḥ-prāmāṇya-vādins (S 11.7) is untenable because fruitful activity may stem from even false cognitions (NM 150) also it may characterise dream cognitions and yet it is difficult to accept such cognition as true. The only alternative, therefore, is to dispense with any criterion of truth and to maintain that truth is self-revealing (however, there may still be a need for criterion of falsehood for according to some version of svataḥ-prāmāṇya-vāda, like Advaitins and Mīmāmsakas though truth is self-revealing falsehood is not).

S 10.17 (ii) The recognition of fruitful activity as a criterion of truth leads according to svataḥ-prāmāṇya-vādins to infinite regress (anavasthā).[16] The recognition amounts according to svataḥ-prāmāṇya-vādins to saying that the truth of one cognition is ascertained by means of another cognition and the truth of this latter cognition by third cognition and so on ad infinitum. Thus on the criterion of fruitful activity truth could never be known. This is contrary to our experience for, truth is constantly known and such knowledge can only be accounted for by saying that truth reveals itself.

S 10.18 This argument reveals a confusion between an activity and cognition. When it is said that we could know the truth of a cognition by checking to see if it could give fruitful results, it is not intended that fruitful result is counted as a cognition. The question of truth or falsity, therefore, does not arise. However, this is not the line of argument that the parataḥ-prāmāṇya-vādins (Naiyāyikas) employ. They try to meet this charge of infinite regress by saying that a cognition which is used in knowing the truth of another cognition need not itself be known to be true. In other words, according to them there is no need to know that truth of a cognition in knowing the truth of another cognition. Mohanty (1969:220) represents the Naiyāyikas' position thus :

> The knowledge which apprehends the truth of another knowledge may be one whose truth has not been ascertained. K_2 may ascertainment the truth of K_1, even if the truth of K_2 has not been ascertained. There is, therefore, no infinite regress.

Even this rejoinder of Naiyāyikas to svatah prāmāṇya-vāda contains the same confusion that is contained in the svatah prāmāṇya-vādins' charge, namely, the confusion between the cognition and an activity. Thus neither the svatah prāmāṇya-vādins' charge nor the paratah-prāmāṇya-vādins' rejoinder is helpful in establishing the svatah prāmāṇya-vādin's dismissal of the need of any criterion of truth.

S 10.19 (iii) Mutual dependence (anyonyāśraya) : The svatah prāmāṇya-vādins argue that the criterion of fruitful activity will not do also for another reason, namely that the criterion leads to the fallacy of mutual dependence (anyonyāśraya). There cannot be a knowledge of the truth of a cognition unless there is fruitful activity and there cannot be fruitful activity unless there is a knowledge of truth of a cognition.[17] As Chatterjee (1939:91) puts it "The knowledge of the validity (truth) of knowledge is said to be conditioned by successful activity, which in turn depends on the knowledge of validity (truth)." It is not clear in what sense successful activity depends on the knowledge of a truth of the relevant cognition. If it means, as is very likely, that truth precedes fruitful activity it is unobjectionable but to say that truth precedes our knowledge of truth (which is a triviality) is very different from saying that *our knowledge of truth* precedes fruitful activity. It is the latter that might be said to involve us in anyonyāśraya and certainly not the former. For strictly speaking fruitful activity is the criterion of our knowledge of truth, and not of truth itself, even though loosely it is so spoken about at times. It is only because no clear distinction is made between truth and knowledge in the Indian tradition in general and in the theories of criteria of knowledge in particular that both svatah-prāmāṇya-vādins and paratah-prāmāṇya-vādins are led to talk about anyonyāśraya in connection with the criterion of fruitful activity (TS 35; Vp 143). The Naiyāyikas' own attempt at escaping the above charge of mutual dependence is very different and unsuccessful as can be seen from its discussion below (SS 11.67).

S 10.20 (iv) Vicious circle (cakraka) ; This argument can be stated as follows : Fruitful activity leads to knowledge of the truth of a cognition, knowledge of the truth of that cognition leods to knowledge of the special quality (guna) of the casual conditions of that cognition, and the knowledge of the special quality (guṇa) of casual conditions ieads to the knowledge of the truth of that cognition which in turn leads to fruitful activity.[18].

S 10.21 From what we have said about the relationship between utpatti, jñapti and prakāśa (S 10.5) it should be clear that this argument is a hotchpotch of utpatti and jñapti. However, if one tries to omit reference to utpatti (*i.e.*, to special quality (guṇa) of casual conditions) and keeps merely to epistemological terms then this argument reduces itself to a case of anyonyāśraya; fruitful activity leads to the knowledge of truth (of a cognition) and knowledge of truth leads to fruitful activity. Thus reduced it can be handed in the same way (iii) above.

Notes and References

1. tadevam sarvapramāṇānām svataḥ prāmāṇye siddhe. . . vede tu pranetuḥ puruṣasyābhāvāt doṣāśankaiva na pravartate vakradhīnatvāddoṣāṇām. NM 144.
2. vadikamīśvaroktatvātsarvameva pramāṇam. TS 62. NM 158.
3. Even though the Naiyāyikas are supposed to hold that Vedic statements are known to be true extrinsically it is not clear in what way they are so known. Their usual criterion of samvādi-pravṛtti (fruitful activity) is not applicable to them, it is applicable only to ordinary statements. We cannot say, therefore, they are known to be true because they lead to fruitful activity. NM (158) clearly says that their truth is known independently of fruitful activity. Does this mean that parataḥ-pramāṇya-vāda of the Naiyāyikas is limited only to ordinary (non-vedic, laukika) statements ? One may try to maintain parataḥ-pramāṇya-vada in respect of Vedic statements as Athalye (1974:353) does by saying that they are known to be true because they are authored by God. The truth of a statement is thus sought to be known with reference to something external (God) to the statement itself. But such an attempt will not do because by the same reasoning even

svataḥ-pramāṇya-vādin will have to be regarded as parataḥ-pramāṇya-vādins for according to svataḥ-pramāṇya-vādins the very conditions that giye rise to our awareness of a (true) cognition makes us aware of its truth. In other words, in producing our awareness of a cognition, the causal conditions also produce our knowledge of its truth. But surely the causal conditions of our awareness of a cognition are external to the cognition itself, and the truth of that cognition will have to be held to be known externally in so far as it is known with reference to such conditions. See S 11.7.

4. The terms 'svatastva-vādin' and 'paratastva-vādin are used by C. Bhattacharya (1975-214), they mean respectively an advocate of the view that the truth value of a statement is known intrinsically and an advocate of the view that the truth value of a statement is known extrinsically.

5. For example, the Advaita-vedāntins and Prābhākaras are both svataḥ-prāmāṇya vādins and svataḥ-prakāśa vādins but the Bhaṭṭas and the followers of Murari Misra though svataḥ prāmāṇya vādins are yet prataḥ-prakāśa vādins. Again the Naiyāyikas are parataḥ-prāmāṇya vādins and also parataḥ-prakāśa vādins; but the Baudhas are parataḥ-prāmāṇya-vadins. Mohanty 1966:3. See Satprakasananda 1974:111-2.

6. yathārthopalabdhih svarūpāvasthitebhya eva kārakebhyo avakalpata iti na guṇakalpanāyai prabhavati. NM 148.

7. anumāne ca yaiva pakṣadharmānvayādisāmagrī *jñāasya* janikā saiva prāmāṇya-kāraṇatvena dṛṣṭā. NM 148.

It should be noted that this is rather a strange and unsual way of using the term 'condition, for pakṣa-dharmatā-jñāna, vyāpti etc. are the elements of inference and can hardly be regarded as conditions of inference. And in any case even if one talks of conditions of inference as W.E. Johnson (1964:7-10) does (where he talks of epistemic and constitutive conditions of inference), such condition will be only condition in epistemological words not in a causal sense as condition of perceptual statements are supposed to be by the traditional Indian thinkers (for example, conditions of perceptual statement are good bright light etc.). One my say, therefore, there is a confusion here between causal conditions and epistemological conditions.

8. NM 148, 157-8; TD 63.

9. Even though Mohanty gives the impression that prakāśa-vāda is concerned with any cognition true or false, in actual practice he limits it to true cognitions only. (Mohanty 1966:3,8).

10. SM 136; Mohanty 1966-8,11; Satprakasananda 1974:112; Matilal 1968a:126.

11. However, svataḥ-prāmāṇya-vāda of the followers of Kumarila Bhaṭṭa and Murāri Miśra conjoins svataḥ-siddha-vāda with parataḥ-prakāśa-vāda. The parataḥ-prakāśa-vdāa is the thesis that the awareness of a cognition is dependent on another cognition but not on itself. For instance, one becomes aware of the cognition of a *j*ar by means of inferential cognition according to Bhaṭṭas (SM 136; Satprakasananda 1974:112; Mohanty 1966:8), and by introspectiive cognition (anuvyavasāya) according to Murāri Miśra (SM 136; Mohanty 1968:11).

12. SM 136 NM ;157; Satprakasananda 1974:110; Mohanty 1966:6; Devarāja 1972:112-3.

13. saṁvadipravṛtyanukūlam. tadati tatprakārakajñanatvaṃ prāmāṇyam "Valid knowledge is that knowledge regarding something possessing a particular attribute, which has that attribute as its feature (prakāra), which is conducive to successful efforts." 143. Translated by Madhavananda 1972:144.

14. pramātvamanadhigatābādhitārthaviṣayakajñanatvam. "... valid knowledge would mean that knowledge which has for its object something that is not already known and is uncontradicted". VP 4. Translated by Madhavananda 1972-5.

15. nanu kṣaṇikatvātkālāntare jñānameva nāsti kasya prāmāṇaṃ niścinumaḥ. "A judgement has a very short span of life. If we fail to determine its validity during its existence how will it be possible for us to do the same Later on ? It ceases to exist at that time. Hence the truth of cannot to be determined." NM 158. Translated by J.V. Bhattacharya 1978:359.

16. NM 159; Chatterjee 1939:94-5; Mohanty 1966:63.

17. tanniścayātpravṛttiḥ syātpravṛttestadviniścayaḥ. "The determination of the truth o! the udgement is the prerequisite condition of movement and such movement leads up to the determination of the truth of the said judgement" NM 151. Translated by J.V. Bhattacharya 1978:344.

18. tatra prāmāṇyavadhāraṇapūrvikayāṃ pravṛttau kāraṇaguṇaniścheyaprāmāṇyacarcābdacakraka-krakacacadhyaprasangastadavastha eva. ". . .The movement of a person helps one to acquire the definite knowledge of the truth of the impelling judgement, its truth leads up to the determination of the special good quality of its cause, the recognition of such good quality helps the ascertainment of the truth of the judgement and such determination of truth impels one to move. Therefore, it is a clear instance of reasoning in a vicious circle." NM 153. Translated by J.V. Bhattacharya 1978:342-3.

11

VAIDIKA ŚABDA AND CRITERIA OF TRUTH (II)

S 11.1 The account given in the preceding chapter, of the positive and negative arguments in favour of svatah-prāmāṇya-vāda also contains a brief evaluation and criticism of those arguments. The traditional criticism of svatah-prāmāṇya-vāda does not of course coincide with my criticism. This can be seen from the following summary of the traditional criticism of svatah-prāmāṇya-vāda (by paratah-prāmāṇya-vādins).

(i) The truth of cognition cannot be self-revealing because there are cognitions in the case of which we are doubtful about the truths.[1]

(ii) That a cognition does not reveal its own truth is also shown by perceptual judgements whose truth depends upon sense object contact.[2]

(iii) The argument that the thesis of self-validity follows from the momentary character will not do because even according to Mīmāṃsakas the falsity of a cognition is known extrinsically.[3] If the falsity of cognition be known extrinsically despite the momentary character of that cognition why not the truth also extrinsically ?

S 11.2 These arguments are cogent even though (ii) needs to be separated from the traditional psychology and restated differently. All in all, therefore, the thesis of self-validity does not hold as an account of our knowledge of the truth of all (known) cognitions; at best it can hold of a small segment of cognitions, namely, what are today called analytic statements.

S 11.3 Some distinguished thinkers like Matilal, Deutsch and Randle give significantly different accounts of svatah-prāmāṇya-vāda. According to them svatah-prāmāṇya-vāda means not that the truth of a cognition is self-manifesting but only that a cognition is to be treated as true until it is proved otherwise (Matilal 1968b: 322-3; Deutsch 1969:87[4]; Randle 1976:51). Such an account of svatah-prāmāṇya-vāda is limited by these authors, either explicitly or implicitly, to empirical cognitions (Randle 1976:51; Mohanty 1966:2-3). The Vedic cognitions are excluded from its perview on the ground that they are eternally true (trikālika abādhita) and their truth is self-manifested (Randle 1976:51; Mohanty 1966:2-3). It is not clear what textual evidence Mohanty and Randle have in mind in giving this version of svatah-prāmāṇya-vāda but at least Deutsch refers to vedanta-paribhaṣa (Chapter VI p. 143-9) in support of his interprepretation. However, as far as I can see Chapter VI of Vedānta-paribhāṣā lends no support to his interpretation. In fact, something is amiss in such an interpretation, is also indicated by S. Murty's (1974:307) objection to svatah-prāmāṇya-vāda, namely, that a man may think that he knowns that p and yet that p may turn out to be false. It is a matter of common experience that cognition strikes us as true but subsequently turns out to be false. This fact could not be an objection to svatah-prāmāṇya-vāda if it were to be interpreted in the manner it is done by Randle, Matilal and Deutsch. I conclude, therefore, that more faithful iuterpretation of svatah-prāmāṇya-vāda is as I have suggested above, and thus interpreted, it is open to the objection raised above and hence, is on the whole an untenable theory.

S 11.4 Theory of extrinsic truth (paratah-prāmāṇya-vāda) : The concepts of utpatti, jñapti and prakāśata are relevant also in the case of pratah-prāmāṇya-vāda. Fortunately the possibili;y of the confusion between them is considerably less in this case. The dstinction between the first two that is utpatti and jñapti is kept very clear. A true cognition is produced not by normal conditions but by an additional circumstance, namely, excellence (guna).[5] This is the utpatti vāda of paratah-prāmāṇya-vādins. Their ñapti-vāda is that a cognition is known to be true not through that cognition itself, but through successful activity to which it leads.[6] In other words, the test or criterion of truth for paratah-pramanya-vadins is successful activity (Mohanty 1966:47-48). This may sound like pragmatism but such an impression is far from truth. The pragmatic theory of truth like the correspondence theory and coherence theory is a theory regarding the nature of truth, as I have emphasised already (S 10.2). The nature of truth is something very different from the criterion of truth. Paratah-prāmāṇya-vāda adopts a pragmatic approach only with regard to the criterion of truth and not with regard to the nature of truth. And this it does because it holds that successful activity is a consequence of truth (NBh 1.1.1).

S 11.5 As for prakāśata, svatah-prāmāṇya-vāda can go with svatah-prakaśa-vada or paratah-prakaśa-vāda. While the Naiyāyikas are both paratah-prāmāṇya vādins and paratah-prakāśa vādins, the Bhāṭṭas are svatah-prāmāṇya-vādins, even though they are also paratah-prakaśa-vadins. I confine my attention in this context to Naiyāyikas' version of paratah-prakāśa-vāda. The Naiyāyikas' paratah-prakāśa-vāda would maintain that we are aware of cognition because of another cognition, namely, introspection or after cognition (anuvyavasāya) *i.e.*, unlike svatah-prakāśa-vāda one has to go beyond the cognition in order to be aware or it. An obvious objection to this view comes from the Advaitins (Satprakasananda 1974:112; Devaraja 1972:113), namely, if a cognition comes to be known through an introspective cognition (anuvyavasāya), the introspective cognition will have to be known through still another introspective cognition and so on ad infinitum. The Naiyāyikas' reply is that the introspective cognition comes to be known intrinsically and not by another introspective cognition. Thus the Naiyāyika is led to compromise his theory by allowing certain exceptions. Another class of cognitions which are accepted by the Naiyāyikas from an extrinsic criterion of truth are those which are about the essential properties of an object (dharma) (Mohanty 1966:54; See fn 103; S 11.7).

S 11.6 The Naiyayikas offer no positive arguments in support of their paratah-prāmāṇya-vāda. All their arguments are indirect in the sense that they are employed either in the refutation of the opposite thesis of svatah-prāmāṇya-vāda or in meeting the objections raised by the advocates of that thesis. Three of them belonging to the first type have already been mentioned in considering the objections to svatah-prāmāṇya-vāda (S 11.1). These are : (i) As there are some cognitions(s) about truth of which we are doubtful; the truth of cognition cannot be self-revealing; (ii) the perceptual judgements which are characterised by sense-object contact imply that a cognition does not reveal its own truth and (ii) The momentary character of a cognition does not support the self-validity of a cognition because even according to Mīmāṃsakas falsity of a cognition is known extrinsically. One of the arguments belonging to the second type (*i.e.*, the one in meeting the opponent's objections) deserves notice here. This is the argument which the Naiyāyikas employ in meeting the Mīmāṃsakas' charges of mutual dependence (anyonyāśraya) and vicious circle (cakraka) stated earlier (SS 10.19-20). The Naiyāyikas give a common rebuttal of these two charges as follows : There are to kinds of objects, namely, transcendental (adṛṣṭa) and empirical (dṛṣṭa). In the case of transcendental objects our knowledge of truth precedes fruitful activity but in the case of empirical objects fruitful activity precedes our knowledge of truth, so there is really no anyonyāśraya.[7] The two statements 'our knowledge of truth precedes fruitful activity' and 'fruitful activity precedes our knowledge of truth' refer to different objects to 'transcendental object in the first case to empirical objects in the second case. In the case of transcendental objects truth is known not by means of fruitful activity but by means of reason and reflection.[8]

S 11.7 The Naiyāyikas do not explain how the same argument takes care of vicious circle but as I have pointed out above (S 10.21) the charge of vicious circle really coincides in its epistemological import with that of mutual dependence. Hence we accept the Naiyāyikas' claim that the same rebuttal applies to both the charges. It may be noted that this rebuttal implies that the criterion of fruitful activity is limited to empirical statements. This does not mean that paratah-pramanya-vada is limited to empirical objects for even employment of reason in ascertaining the truth of Vedic statements makes such statements paratah-prāmāṇya according to NM (160). Athalye (1974:353), on the other hand, thinks that paratah-prāmāṇya-vāda is maintained even in the case of vedic statements by reference to the authorship of God, (fn 10.3) though not by reference to the criterion of fruitful activity. But of course these are futile attempts at saving paratah-prāmāṇya-vāda in respect of Vedic statements; for, 'reason' can hardly be said to be a criterion of truth external to the given statement. Even the mere inspection of its import involves it. In fact, the criterion of reason is implicit in contrary thesis of svatah-prāmāṇya-vāda and cannot be a distinctive part of paratah-prāmāṇya-vāda. The employment of reason of course is involved in all rational activities, therefore, in the employment of criterion of fruitful activity. But this does not make it necessarily an independent criterion, and, if it is made an independent criterion, it can be only within the context of svatah-prāmāṇya-vāda and not of paratah-prāmāṇya-vāda despite the Naiyayikas' claim. Similarly reference to the authoring of God cannot save paratah-prāmāṇya vāda in the case of Vedic statements for authorship of God cannot be the criterion for human knowledge, for example, if it is said that a statement S_1 is true because of the statement S_2, namely, that S_2 is authored by God. The question of truth of S_2 still remains : How do we know that S_1 is authored by God. Moreover, if divine authorship also means that God creates Vedic truths rather than transmits them then the fact that the truths are created by God does not mean that they are known to human beings (fn 10.3).

S 11.8 NM (158) gives the impression that the distinction between transcendental objects and empirical objects also helps us to meet the charge of infinite regress (anavasthā). But it is not clear to me how that distinction can play any role in meeting that charge. However, I have pointed out on independent grounds (S 10.18) that the charge is untenable.

S 11.9 That, according to paratah-pramanya-vadins (*i.e.*, Naiyāyikas), the criterion (of saṃvādi-pravṛtti) of knowledge is external to the statement whose truth value is being ascertained, is obvious enough. However, what is not obvious is the Nyāya position on the closely related question, namely, the question of the nature of truth. As has been already remarked (S 1.2), the Naiyayikas share the same definition of truth with their rivals, namely, svatah-prāmāṇya-vādins. Both the rival camps subscribe to the view that truth is tadvati tatprakarako anubhavaḥ. ("A cognition which has, for its subject, something which possesses the character which that cognition has for its predicate is true cognition." (TS 35; VP 143). How is one to interpret this definition ? Authors like S. Murty (1974:307), Matilal (1968a:16) take it to mean to correspond with reality. They thus ascribe to it a variety of correspondence theory of truth. But then on the same reasoning svatah-prāmāṇya-vādins (Mīmāṃsakas and Advaitins) too would have to be regarded as realists. But there seems to be no special enthusiasm amongst the traditional writers to describe the Mīmaṃsakas and Advaitins as realists. Besides Hiriyanna (1973:308-9) goes to the extent of saying that paratah-prāmāṇya-vāda of Naiyāyakas really goes counter to their realistic position and Chatterjee (1939:113) maintains that Naiyāyikas' position of paratah-prāmāṇya-vāda embraces all the three classical western theories of nature of truth, namely, the coherence theory, correspondence theory and pramatic theory. What is it then that prompts the authors like S. Murty and Matilal to ascribe a correspondence theory of truth to the Naiyāyikas ? It cannot be the Naiyāyikas' view of the criterion of truth since that is held to be either incompatible with realistic position (as contended by Hiriyanna) or comprehensive enough to accommodate not only correspondence theory but also coherence theory and pragmatic theory as well (as suggested by Chatterjee). Nor can it be the Nyāya definition of truth since the same definittion is shared by the rival camp of svatah-prāmāṇa-vadins. The Nyāya definition of truth can be taken to mean correspondence theory only if one is prepared to ascribe to Mīmaṃsakas and Advaitins a similar or the same realistic position. As far as my knowledge goes such readiness is not much in evidence in primary or secondary writings. Mohanty (1966:75-9) makes an effort to reconcile these two opposing theories of svatah-pramanya-vāda and paratah-prāmāṇya-vāda but his efforts is so unconvincing that we need not pursue it here. Even though Matilal ascribes a correspondence theory of truth to Nyāya he (Matilal 1968b:332) still thinks that the Nyaya (especially Gangeśa's) conception of truth is very different from Tarski's semantic definition of truth. Whether or not Gangeśa's theory can be construed along the lines of Tarski's semantic theory is a debatable point. But even if Gangeśa's theory is in substance different from Tarsks's it would be so, not because of the sort of reason that Matilal (1968b:332)[9] adduces but for rather different reasons, into these I do not wish to go here.

1. pramātvaṃ na svato grāhyaṃ, saṃśayānupapattiḥ. "The validity of knowledge is not self-evident, because in that case doubt cannot be explained." BP 136. Translated by Madhavananda 1977:221. NM 157.

2. prāmāṇyamindriyavyāpāralabdhajanmanā pratyekṣeṇa parichchidhyata. "The judgement is true in such a limited sense because it is learnt that it owes its existence to the sense-object contact." NM 155. Translated by J.V. Bhattacharya 1978-351.

   tatra pratyakṣe viśeṣaṇavadviśeṣyasaṃnikarṣo guṇaḥ. "The good property, for perceptual knowledge, is sense-contact with such a sustantive as possesses the predicated character." TD 63. Translated by C. Bhattacharya 1975:200.

3. aprāmāṇyamapi bādhakapratyādinā kālāntare kasya niścinumaḥ. But its falsehood is extrinsically determined. A judgement is determined to be false only when the truth of its contradictory one is known as true at a later period." NM 158. Translated by J.V. Bhattacharya 1978:459.

4. It is because Deutsch (1969:86-7) interprets svataḥ-prāmāṇya-vāda in this way that he is led to say that svataḥ-prāmāṇya-vāda is a kind of perverse pragmatism and that it resembles in some respects Popper's (1968:84, 86-7) falsification theory.

5. pramāyā guṇajanyatvamutpattau pratastvam. "The fact that valid knowledge is caused by a good property (in the conditions of knowledge) is what constitutes the indirectness of its origination (utpattu paratastvam)." TD 63. Translated C. Bhattacharya 1975:200. NM 157.

6. . . . arthakriyājñānātpramāṇyaniścaya. . "the knowledge of the practical efficiency of an object assures us of the truth of the impellent judgement." NM 160. Translated by J.V. Bhattacharya 1978:364. TD 63; SM 136.

7. tatrādṛṣṭe viṣaye prāmāṇyaniścayapūrvikāyāḥ pravṛtterabhyugamānnetaretarāśrayaṃ cakrakaṃ vā, dṛṣṭeviṣaye hyanirṇītaprāmāṇya evārthasaṃśayātpravṛttirūpamanarthasaṃśayācca nivatyātmakaṃ vyavahāramārabhāmāno dṛśyate lokaḥ. . ."Regarding the transcendental object they are of opinion that when they are definitely known to be true the people move for their atiainment. The fallacies of mutual dependence, vicious circle, etc., do not affect their thesis. But with regard to the ordinary objects of every day experience a person moves for their attainment when he does not determine the truth of the impellent judgement but thinks that the truth of it is highly probable." NM 158. Translated by J.V. Bhattacharya 1978:360.

8. tasmādadṛṣṭapuruṣārthapadopadeśi mānaṃ manoṣibhiravaśyaparīkṣaṇīyam. prāmāṇayamasya parato niranāyi ceti. "In fine, the truth of the śāstras which deal with the means to the transcendental ends should be critically examined. We have arrived at the conclusion that the truth of such śāstras is extrinically but not intrinsically determined." NM1 60. Translated by J.V. Bhattacharya 1978:366.

9. Just to give the passing limbs of the situation Matilal (1968b:332) confuses pramātva with truth. Perhaps some sense can be made of his (Matilal's) statements that pramātva belongs to cognitive states but certainly truth cannot be said to belong to such states.

12

CONCLUSION

S 12.1 It should be clear from the foregoing chapters that scriptural testimony constitutes the very heart of my treatment of śabda pramāṇa. Even though Indian philosophical tradition by and large recognises scriptural testimony as the most important variety of śabda pramāṇa and, hence, a vital source of knowledge, it does not mean that this traditional position is acceptable to the contemporary mind. In fact it has come in for very severe attack by what constitutes to day an important phase of contemporary philosophy. This phase may be broadly described as logical empiricism, though it has many variants. This attack is based on a certain theory of meaning and we must begin with the principle underlying this theory. This is the so called principle of verification. It was initially stated by M. Schlick and some other members of the Vienna Circk, and was popularised by Ayer's account of it in his *Language Truth and Logic*. Schlick (1949:148) puts it in a nutshell : "The meaning of a proposition is the method of its verification." But it is Ayer who brings out the various facets of the verification principle (pv)[1] in a most lucid fashion. He makes a distinction between a statement and a proposition : a statement is what is expressed by an indicative sentence.[2] A proposition, on the other hand, is a statement which satisfies the principle of verification. This means that the set of propositions is a proper subset of the set of statement. Making use of this distinction, Ayer (1946:9) gives the first of his formulations of the verifiability principle by saying : "a statement is said to be literally meaningful if and anly if it is either analytic or empirically verifiable." We may call this formulation pv1. A statement is said to be analytic "if it is true solely in virtue of the meanings of its constituent symbols, and cannot, therefore, be either confirmed or refuted by any fact of experience" (Ayer 1946:16). What Ayer really means is that the truth value (not just truth) of an analytic statement depends solely on the meaning and definition of its terms so that an analytic statement may be either true or false or, more accurately, analytically true or analytically false. An analytic statement is vacuous or tautological in the sense that it gives no information about the world. In other words, it has absolutely no empirical content. But the more significant class of statements in this context consists of those which are said to be empirically verifiable. In an attempt to explain what is meant by "empirically verifiable," Ayer introduces some further distinctions. One of these is between practical verifiability and verifibility in principle. A statement is said to be practically verifiable if in actual practice we can verify it. It is verifiable in principle if we know what sort of observation would verify it even though at present we do not know how to go about in order to make such observations. The verification principle requires not practical verifiability but only verifiability in principle.

S 12.2 Another distinction that Ayer (1946:9) introduce is the one between strong and weak verification. A statement is strongly verifiable if and only if it could be conslusively established. On the other hand, it is weekly verifiable if experience can render it probable. What the principle of verification requires is not strong verifiability but only weak verifiability. But the question arises whether strong verifiability is possible at all even in principle, for Ayer himself allows that all empirical statements are hypothesis. This means that they can never be conclusively confirmed nor conclusively confuted, further experience being always relevant to them. Ayer tries to wriggle out of this inconsistency by bringing in the concept of 'basic proposition.' A basic proposition is one which refers solely to the context of a single experience and the occurrence of the relevant experience conclusively verifies it. Examples of such a proposition are "I have a toothache now", "I see a red patch there" etc. These seem to be statements about one's private and subjective experiences and have no objective import. They may, therefore, be said to be incorrigible. Many people would object to regarding these as empirical statements. If they are not so regarded then strong verifiability becomes irrelevant and the principle of verifiability would only need weak verifiability. 'Strong verifiability' would be needed by pV only if basic propositions are included under empirical propositions.

S 12.3 Ayer (1946:11) further clarifies weak verifiability by introducing the notion of an observation statement. An observation statement is one which records actual or possible observation. The difference between a basic statement and an observation statement seems to be that while the former is subjective in import; the latter is objective in import; *i.e.*, the observations that the latter records, are publicly available. A statement is weakly verifiable if some observation statements can be deduced from it in conjunction with some other statements without being deducible from those other statements alone.

S 12.4 The verification principle as stated above in pv_1 really ends up with allowing meaning to any statements at all including metaphysical ones. Where O is an observation statement and S any statement at all, O is deducible from S in conjunction with "$S \rightarrow O$". This would mean that S is literally meaningful even if it is a metaphysical statement. Ayer tries to avoid this disastrous consequence by reformulating PV_1 as :

(PV_2) A statement is literally significant if it is either analytic or directly or indirectly verifiable. It is directly verifiable if either it is itself an observation statement or entails in conjunction with other observation statement(s) at least one observation statement which is not deducible from these other observation statement (s) alone. A statement is indirectly verifiable if it satisfies the following two conditions : (1) In conjunction with some other premisses if it entails one or more directly verifiable statements which are not deducible from these other premisses alone. (2) These other premisses do not include any statement that is not either analytic or directly verifiable or capable of being indirectly established as indirectly verifiable. Ayer (1946 : 13).

S 12.5. It is to be noted that even in the amended version PV_2 is meant to determine literal or cognitive meaning. To say that a statement lacks literal meaning is not to say, as Ayer (1946 : 15) makes it clear, that it lacks other kinds of meaning such as emotive, figurative, etc. But the question is : even as determinant of literal meaning, is pv_2 adequate ? Ayer himself confesses that others, especially metaphysiciants, may not consider it as adequate ; in fact, they may consider it arbitrary. After all the verification principle is a matter of definition or a methodological principle (Ayer 1946 : 16) or a linguistic proposal which is itself neither true nor false (Hempel : 1959 : 125). To define meaning in any worthwhile fashion and classify statements accordingly, the analysis of meaning has to be rooted in something more solid and objective. These are general criticisms of pv_2. Definitions, methodological principles, and linguistic proposals are at least in some cases arbitrary and pv_2 seems to determine meaning just by a fiat. There are specific criticisms also. Some of these are so powerful as to compel revision of pv_2. One such specific criticism may be formulated as follows :

Suppose N is a metaphysical statement and O_1 and O_2 are observation statements. Then "$\sim O_1$ v $(N.O_2)$" is directly verifiable ; for in conjunction with O_1 it entails O_2. So "$\sim O_1$ v$(N.O_2)$" would qualify as literally significant even though it contains a metaphysical statement as its component, (see Hempel 1959 : 112-3). This consequence is obviously unacceptable to positivists themselves.

S 12.6. Another powerful specific criticism is due to Church (see Brown and Watling 1951 : 87). It is that given any three observation statements none of which alone entails the rest, it follows that for any sentence S at all that either it or its negation is literally significant. Suppose that O_1, O_2, and O_3 are such observation statements ; then "$(\sim O_1.O_2)$ v $(O_3. \sim S)$" will be directly verifiable ; for, jointly with O_1 it entails O_3. Further, S is indirectly verifiable, since it along with "$(\sim O.O_2)$ v $(O_3 \sim S)$" entails O_2. If it happens that "$(\sim O_1.O_2)$ v $(O_3. \sim S)$" entails O_2 by itself, then "$\sim S$" jointly with O_3 entails O_2 so that "$\sim S$" is directly verifiable.

S 12.7. Various attempts have been made to rescue pv_2 from such fatal criticisms. Brown and Watling (1951 : 88-9) for instance, add the following stipulation to pv_2 : "If a statement is molecular then it must not contain any component whose deletion leaves the statement which entails verifiable statements not entailed by the original statement ; or does not entail verifiable statements entailed by the original statement." The purpose of this stipulation is to exclude literally non-sensical statements such as 'the Absolute is perfect'.

S 12.8. Hempel (1959 : 116-7) tries to achieve the same purpose of denying literal significance to metaphysical statements by replacing pv_2 by another principle which is in the same empirical spirit. He calls this principle the Translatability Criterion of Cognitive Meaning and formulates it thus : "A sentence has cognitive meantng if and only if it is translatable into empiricist language." The logical vocabulary of an empiricit language and its rules of formation are the usual ones, namely, those to be found in *Principii Mathematica*. The non-logical vocabulary consists of observation predicates, *i.e.*, expressions expressing observable characteristics (a property or a relation) whose presence or absence is ascertained by observation. It is obvious that an empiricist language by its very nature excludes literally non-sensical statements. Translatability seems to assure literal significance.

S 12.9. However, even such attempts to save an empiricist criterion of meaning, especially pv_2, are found to be unsatisfactory for various reasons.[3] It is not necessary for me to go into these reasons. What is important is that inspite of the various criticisms against pv_2 or its variants, there is a strong tendency amongst a large number of philosophers to deny the possibility of a non-empiricist criterion of meaning. It is a matter of solid conviction for them that the basis for any theory of meaning can only be some variant of an empiricist criterion of meaning, if not pv_2 itself. And they insist that since religious statements (which scriptural statements are) do not satisfy such a criterion, they are bereft of literal significance.

S 12.10. Attempts have been made to loosen the hold of this conviction by philosophers. According to these philosophers[4] what is wrong with pv (or some other empiricist criterion of meaning) is not its precise formulation or some other detail, but its very spirit. An empiricist criterion of meaning, whatever its form, just will not do for them, and they favour, implicitly or explicitly, an alternative criterion which they think is more adequate and accommodates scriptural (and other religious) statements. Let me take a brief look at some notable attempts in this regard.

S 12.11. Such attempts may be said to fall into two broad categories : (A) Those which derive their inspiration from the traditional approach to religious statements, and (B) those which derive directly or indirectly from the views of later Wittgenstein. Let me first consider the attempts of category A.

As representatives of category A we may mention, among others, Broad (1963 169), Price (1969 : 480), Crombie (1963 : 292-3, 288), Mitchel (1963 : 280), Alston (1964 : 80-1), and Hick (1979 : 68-9). The main thrust of such thinkers is to argue for a theory of meaning which is comprehensive enough to accommodate especially religious statements (and of course, aesthetic and ethical statements) within meaningful discourse. They argue for the meaningfulness of religious statements either by putting them on a par with empirical statements and claiming verifiability for them, though not in terms of sense experience ; or by claiming uniqueness for such statements and proposing a special sort of justification for them. The former approach is adopted by Broad (1963 : 169), Price (1969 : 480), Mitchel (1963 : 280) and Crombie (1963 : 292-3). The latter approach is favoured by Alston (1964 : 80-1) and Hick (1979 : 68-9). However, the difference between these two groups of thinkers tends to be mostly verbal. Basically the accounts given by both groups for the meaningfulness of religious discourse are along similar lines.

S 12.12. Broad (1963 : 169), Price (1969 : 480), Crombie (1963 : 288), and Mitchel (1963 : 280) admit the distinctive character of religious statements as against empirical statements and yet, as a sop to the current positivist craze, even go to the extent of allowing verifiability to them. But the verifiability thus allowed to them is not in terms of sense experience, but in terms of experience obtained through transcendental faculties like revelation, mystic intuition, and scriptural authority.[5] They contend that even these transcendental sources are genuinely cognitive and that the positivist is merely being perverse in restricting cognitive meaning to what he calls empirical and analytical statements. They point out that all great mystics of the world have had similar experiences, and that the basic identity of their transcendental experiences can be quite an acceptable source not only of meaning but also of validity of religious statements. Similar claims are made on behalf of revelation. Revelation is the process in which God imparts transcendental knowledge to a chosen few. The concept of revelation thus involves the concept of grace (S 9.2). How can, what is imparted in such a unique and sublime fashion be suspect ? On the contrary it constitutes, these thinkers insist, the highest kind of verification and justification. Before it, verification in terms of sense experience pales into insignificance.

S 12.13. The other two thinkers who advocate meaningfulness of religious statements, namely, Alston (1964 : 80-1) and Hick (1979 : 68-9), emphasise the uniqueness of religious discourse but prefer not to talk of verifiability in relation to it. They would rather talk about the justification of such discourse. The justification for these thinkers also comes essentially from a transcendental faculty, whether it is mystical institution or revelation or scriptural authority. But their refusal to apply the terms 'verifiability', 'verifi cation' etc. to religious statements is, as remarked above, merely a terminological decision. Their basic position regarding the nature and validity of religious statements remains the same as that of the first group of thinkers.

S 12.14. What guarantee is there that the mystics and morally enlightened persons are correctly reporting their experiences ? Is there really agreement about their experiences ? Could agreement not have been faked ? To questions such as these the answer of thinkers of the first group under category A is that mystic experience and moral insight is not the privilege of only a few. It is attainable by every one provided he undergoes the necessary training and discipline. Such a discipline is unusually hard and prolonged, and failures in its pursuit are frequent and widespread. But those few who perservere enough will finally qualify for receiving religious and moral insight, and will serve as source of meaningfulness and justification of religious discourse. Actually Price (1969.480) likens the training and discipline required for transcendental experience to a system of physical exercises or a system of memory training, If the trainee fails, he has only to try again until he attains the required level of proficiency. Mitchel (1963 : 280) compares a religious person to a stranger whose statement ("I am on your side") we are led to accept because of a certain pattern in his behaviour even though this evidence may not be conclusive. But the important thing is that the evidence is also not conclusively against the stranger's statement. Likewise, a religious person's statement like "God is merciful" is to be accepted because we do have some evidence of God's mercy to his creatures, though it may not be conclusive. Crombie (1963 : 292-3) goes even further and holds that religious claims can be accepted even in the face of apparently contrary evidence at the empirical level. The clash of religious claims with evidence at the phenomenal level is, according to him, due to our finitude and we may not be able to resolve it. Nevertheless that is no reason for not accepting religious claims ; just as our inability to get into the position of deciding what Julius Caesar had for breakfast before he crossed the Rubicon is no reason for our not accepting that he did have breakfast on that occasion. Thus, for Crombie also religious statements are analogous to statements of facts and justifiable in terms of experience though such experience is of non-sensuous character. Such thinkers (for example Mitchel 1978 : 54) try to strengthen their plea for the meaningfulness of religious statements by referring to the scientific language of theoretical terms like 'current', 'atom', 'particle', 'wave' 'field' etc. They point out that science employs such terms even though literally speaking there is nothing that they name and hence their use can only be regarded as analogical. If so, why can we not employ religious expressions even though there is nothing in sensuous experience that directly corresponds to them ? They can also be said to be used analogically as was argued by Aquinas long ago and present day authors (see Hick 1979 : 79-81) and Mitchel (1963 : 280). It is also further argued by these traditionalists that religious statements are compatible with empirical statements and that therefore, they should not be rejected out of hand for want of empirical support.

S 12.15. What can we say of these attempts which try to defend the traditional approach by adding certain contemporary conceptual sophistications ? To put it bluntly, it cannot be said that the traditionalists have succeeded in their case for meaningfulness of religious statements. In order to appreciate this blunt remark, it must be emphasised that for the proponents of PV and of other empiricist criteria of meaning, what is at issue is the literal or cognitive sense, and not meaning in general. For, the contemporary empiricists are not only willing but also eager to concede that there are other kinds of meaning than literal (S 12.5). They emphasise that religious and other non-empirical statements may have emotive, figurative, or analogical meaning. What they deny is literal or cognitive meaning. For them literal meaning is directly or indirectly in terms of sense-experience (or in terms of analyticity). The possibility or otherwise of non-sensuous experience is really not in question, even though some logical positivists in the first flush of their enthusiasm might have gone to the extreme of denying such possibility. Even if the possibility of non-sensuous experience is admitted, the question still remains of its cognitive and epistemological status, and it is this status that the empiricists stoutly deny. If we remember this, it can be seen that the traditionalists' arguments in favour of religious statements have little strength. They have all been rebutted in the past and need only to be recounted in passing.

S 12.16. Take for instance the case of mystical experience. There is first of all no conclusive evidence for identity of mystical experiences by different mystics. What is more, there is even the question of the genuineness of such experiences. One may claim to know Brahman as the only reality in a mystical intuition, but another may counter by claiming to know Super-Brahman in a similar fashion. How is one to decide between such conflicting claims ? Surely one of them must be false. But which is genuine and which is false ? There are no acceptable criteria for deciding these questions. Again, it has been argued that the transcendental sources are open to any one if only he tries hard enough and long enough. But how long and how hard ? And what exactly are the details of the training ? Nobody has specified the exact details of the training to be undergone. Let us suppose that somehow the contents of the training are determined. Even after one has completed the hard and long training to the satisfaction of experts, there is no quarantee that one will have the mystical vision. How does one account for the failure ? It will not do to say, after one fails, that one has not tried hard enough and long enough. Such a judgement would be retrospective and not prospective. We need the means of making a prospective judgement. Broad, Pricc, Mitchel. Crombie etc. talk of religious statements being statements of fact, and of their verifiability. But they fail to make intelligible the nature of the facts the religious statements are supposed to express and the kind of verifiability that is supposed to apply to religious statements. Mitchel's comparison (S 12.14) of a religious statement to the stranger's statement will not do, because in the case of the stranger's statement there definite empirical evidence is available which can count for or against ;

and in certain contexts such evidence can even be conclusive. But no empirical evidence can really be said to be in favour or against a religious statement. A religious person will stick to his belief, whatever the empirical evidence.

Similarly, Crombie (1963 : 292-3) also is not right in saying that our inability to find empirical support for religious claims is no reason not to accept them. His comparison of a religious claim with the case of Caesar's breakfast is misconceived ; for even though I myself, removed as I am by this great distance in time, cannot get into the position of *directly* determining the contents of Caesar's breakfast, there are acceptable empirical ways of determining those contents. But there are no acceptable ways of religious claims.

S 12.17. The traditionalists' attempt to strengthen their case from theoretical scientific terms like 'wave', 'particle', etc. is also futile. For, even though such terms do not directly name any single phenomenon, they have a colligating function and serve to unify a certain range of phenomenona. They are, therefore, ultimately rooted in sense experience. Religious terms can hardly be said to be similarly rooted. Nor can they be said to have a colligating function. (But this is not to deny that sense experience may play some role in the meaningfulness of theological predicates. See next section). Similarly the traditionalists' attempts to justify religious statements on the ground of their compatability with empirical statements is in vain. For, compatability can in no sense be regarded as support. The two statements, "2 is an even number" and "Kalidas is a great poet" are obviously compatible. But neither has the slightest tendency to support the other.

S 12.18. Authors like Alston (1967 : 169) and Hick (1979 : 68-9) adopt a less drastic approach than Mitchel to religious terms in general and theological terms in particular. It was noticed above (S 12.14) that Mitchel holds (though wrongly) that theological terms are exactly on the same level as theoretical scientific terms like 'particle', 'wave', etc. As against his view Alston (1967 : 169) and Hick (1979 : 68-9) think that theological predicates are derived from empirical predicates though they go beyond them. A single theological predicate may be derived from one single empirical predicate or more than one such predicates. Two things need to be noted in this regard. First, it is very difficult to explain how exactly a given theological predicate is derived from corresponding empirical predicates and how it transcends those predicates. This difficulty is further aggravated when authors like Alston (1967 : 169) claim that in determining the meaning of theological predicates its empirical content is to be discounted. For, if the meaning of an empirical predicate is primary to that of a theological predicate, as these authors claim, then it is not clear what if any thing, remains of the meaning of theological predicates after they are emptied of their empirical content. The problem is to account for the uniqueness and transcendent character of the significance of theological predicates, and in this task I do not think that authors like Hick and Alston have succeeded. In fact it is doubtful whether this task can at all be achieved by linking theological predicates with empirical predicates.

Second, this attempt at linking theological predicate with empirical predicates is at best an attempt to explain how religious concepts are formed; but explanation of concept-formation is not the same as logical analysis of concepts. The former is the psychologist's, not the philosopher's concern. What the philosopher seeks, or ought to seek, is conceptual analysis. I am not satisfied that the account given by Alston and Hick of theological predicate qualifies as conceptual analysis.

S 12.19 Even supposing that religious terms somehow have a meaning, their meaningfulness would still not guarantee *cognitive* sense of the religious statements in which they figure. It is a common fact that expressions formed out of elements which are obviously meaningful often lack cognitive meaning. For example, the expression "Three is snub-nosed" (when literally considered) can hardly be said to have cognitive meaning, even though there can be no doubt about the meaningfulness of each of its constituent terms. If this is so when the constituent terms are the usual ones; it can be even more so when the constituent terms are unusual or unique as religious terms are. In other words, it would not be correct to infer cognitive meaning of religious statements from just the meaningfulness of their constituent terms (even supposing that such terms have meaning). Besides, the meaning that such terms may have, may not be of the right sort, *i.e.*, the sort that is needed to yield cognitive meaning of statements. It may be, for instance, emotive or metaphorical.

S 12.20 I have so far considered attempts of thinkers of category A (the traditionalists (SS 12.11-19) to loossen the grip of an empiricist criterion of meaning. I will now consider similar attempts made by thinkers of category B (later Wittgenstein and his followers). It is to be noted that though thinkers of category A were fighting against an empiricit criterion of meaning, they did not put forward any explicit and well-developed theory of meaning as an alternative. Whatever theory of meaning they had in mind was only implicit. It is thinkers of category B, especially Wittgenstein, who met this challenge head on, and produced an alternative, fully developed, theory of mraning. It is interesting to remember that Wittgenstein in his early phase (of the *Tractatus*) was himself an advocate of an empiricit theory of meaning. Yet in his later phase (of the *Philosophical Investigations*), he put forward an entirely different theory of meaning on the ground that an empiricist theory of meaning is not satisfactory. This is the theory that the meaning of an expression is the method of its use, not the method of its verification.

S 12.21 The claim that meaning of an expression is its use might give one the impression that the search for meaning of an expression is limited to an *empirical* investigation of the behaviour of that expression in a given language. In other words, one may get the impression that questions of meaning are relative to a given language and that they are empirical in character. Such an impression, however, would be grievously wrong. Wittgenstein is not concerned with events that constitute the history of an expression. He is concerned with the analysis of the concept of meaning. His theory holds irrespective of the peculiarities of different languages. Suppose that he is concerned with clarifying the meaning of the expression, 'the present prince of Wales'. This expression, of course, happens to belong to the English language but the answer Wittgenstein seeks to give in terms of its use is intended to apply not only to this particular expression, but also to every equivalent expression of other languages actual or possible (Malcolm 1967: 334-7). This fact is perhaps better brought out by saying that what Wittgenstein is after is not just the use of an expression, but the *logic* of its use. The aim is conceptual clarification and philosophical illumination, not lexical inventory. This becomes obvious when we notice that Witgenstein links the notion of use to the concepts of *language game* and *form of life*, especially the former. In order to determine the meaning of an expression we must take a comprehensive look at the game that we play with it. Doing so covers linguistic as well as non-linguistic behaviour of the language user (Pitcher 1964:240). Language games are not fixed, nor is there any thing universal about them. They are infinitely diverse and can have nothing more substantial in common than family resemblances. This is as it should be; otherwise the diversity of meaning of the infinitely many expressions of the some and different languages would not be accounted for. Also, fresh language games may arise corresponding to coming into being of new concepts. Similarly, existing language games may disappear corresponding to disappearance of certain concepts. What is important to note about a language game is that it is a rule-regulated activity and in looking for the meaning of an expression we are looking for *the rules* (*i.e.*, the logic) of the game we play by means of that expression.

A form of life is a much more rigid and stable conceptual structure than a language game. Language games, singly or in combination, may enter into the constitution of a form of life. When one is trying to determine the meaning of an expression one is also, therefore, indirectty referring to a form of life via the relevant language game. But a form of life is, as it were, a common denominator of a certain set of language games, and it can contribute little directly to the determination of individual concepts and propositions (which meanings of words and statements are). However, it does contribute significantly to this purpose in an indirect fashion.

S 12.22 This theory of meaning is general enough to apply to all categories of expressions—words, phrases, and statements. It is also comprehensive enough to accommodate every kind of expression that is actually a part of any existing language. Since religious discourse has been vary much a part of almost every natural language, it follows that such discourse is meaningful (Sengupta 1978:34-6). But the crucial question is whether the meaning that is supposed to belong to religious discourse is cognitive. Wittgenstein's later theory of meaning, as far as I know, does not explicitly distinguish between different kinds of meaning. But obviously Wittgenstein implies that the conceptual clarification of religious expressions results in philosophical illumination and this can only mean that the meaning that such expressions have, is of the cognitive variety. If it is not, religious language would not be, amenable to philosophical investigation.

Has Wittgenstein really succeeded in accomodating religious language, including scriptural statements, within meaningful discourse ? Wittgenstein uses the concepts of *language game* and *form of life* so widely and gives them (especially *form of life*) such ultimacy that they become almost vacuous. Any expression of any language can be claimed to be meaningful on his theory. And this goes for poetic and mythological expreesions as well. One may perhaps concede that any expression of any langnage has *some sort* of meaning. But, as remarked above, the crucial question is whether every expression, and therefore, every religious expression can be said to have *cognitive* meaning. Would Wittgenstein claim cognitive meaning for poetic and mythological expressions also ? Is a musical score or an aesthetic expression cognitively meaningful ? The answer, I am afraid, has to be in the negative. As emphasised earlier (S 12.5), those who advocate an empiricist criterion of meaning and hence deny cognitive meaning to religious and scriptural language, do not deny non-cognitive meaning to such language. They only disallow cognitive meaning to it. Human knowledge cannot transcend the categories of our reason and understanding. Whenever it attempts to do so, it gets bogged down in contradictions and paralogisms. as has been repeatedly pointed out in the history of philosophy.[6] But if we keep the limits of the categories of our logic, then surely the claim to knowledge of supra-sensible object, on which the admissibility of religious language essentially rests, becomes untenable. And religious language would have to be denied cognitive status. This is the central point that the empiricists rightly make, whatever their failings.

S 12.23 That we engage in certain linguistic and religious pattern of behaviour is a sociological fact, and therefore, a part of human history. In other words, language games and forms of life are components of human history. To maintain that a certain expression is meaningful because it is tied into these components is to lose sight of the transcendental character of religious discourse. This is what Burke (1978:510-2) tries to emphasis. His point may be paraphrased as follows :

When we speak of religion as a 'form of life' or as a 'language game', we are classifying it in a certain way which people choose or adopt or take up. In other words, we are treating it as one of the products, of human life, and setling ourselves to determine what distinguishes it from other such products. But, for a religious believer the ultimate appeal is not to what is the done-thing within any human society, but to what he accepts as *the will of God or the word of God.*

S 12.24 Statements *about* language games and forms of life, of course, do have cognitive status, because they are empirical. They express empirical (sociological) facts namely, the language games and the forms of life in question. But such statements can hardly be called religious discourse. What constitute religious discourse are those statements which are about some special contents of the forms of life and language games. It is to those that empiricists and their fellow-travellers deny cognitive meaning.

S 12.25 It should be noted that Wittgenstein emphasises the automony of language games and forms of life. This autonomy means that one language-game cannot be reduced to another; nor can one form of life be assimilated to another. In other words, the language of religion cannot be reduced to the language of science or to any other kind of language. Wittgenstein seems to maintain that any attempt to make sense of religion or to validate its claims in non-religious terms is self-defeating, since it amounts to surrendering religious claims altogether (Burke 1978:510-2). But when it is the cognitive status of religious language that is at issue, such a status cannot be established in terms of further religious language. To do so would be just begging the question. The cognitive status of religious language can only be established in terms of language whose cognitive status is beyond question (Cf. Schmidt 1961:97-112). The only kind of language whose cognitive status is beyond question are the language of science and the language of logic; and neither of these languages can accord cognitive credibility to religious language.

S 12.26 What is the upshot of all this on scriptural testimony which, after all, is the central topic of my investigation ? Scriptural testimony consists of statements about transcendental entities. Hence, it is religious language par excellence. Whatever we have said so far about religious language automatically applies to scriptural testimony as well. We have concluded that religious language cannot be accorded cognitive status. The same conclusion must apply to scriptual testimony also. It has been pointed out earlier (S 0.1) the scriptural testimony is traditionally claimed to be a genuine pramāṇa and that it also statisfies the criterion of independence (S 8.8). The knowledge it is supposed to yield is traditiondally believed to be the highest kind of knowledge. Our account of the empiricist criteria of meaning including pv and that of religious language should make it clear that these traditional claims on behalf of scriptural testimony are unacceptable. If scriptural testimony is bereft of cognitive status, it cannot be a source of genuine knowledge. In other words it cannot be a pramāṇa in the true sense of the word, since strictly speaking, no knowledge can be obtained from it. Mundane testimony, of course, is a source of knowledge but it is reducible to other sources, namely, perception and inference.

Notes and References

1. pv is an abbreviation for the verifiability principle in general.
2. Any group of words that is gramatically significant constitutes a sentence according to Ayer (1946:8).
3. Hempel (1959:125-; 6; 128) himself acknowledges the deficiency of his translatability criterion.
4. The criticisms against pv noted above (SS 12.5-6) are needles to say, from those who still keep their faith in an empiricist criterion of meaning, but only argue about how to improve it.
5. Scriptural authority ultimately reduces itself to revelation or intuition.
6. For example, by Hume and Kant apart from the logical positivists, Wittgenstein also declares in the *Tractatus* : whereof we cannot speak, thereof we must be silent.

ADDENDUM

SCRIPTURAL TESTIMONY

S 1. It is clear from the Chapters (VI to XI) that scriptural testimony constitutes the core of my treatement of Śabda pramāṇa. As it has been pointed out (S. 12.1) Indian philosophical traditions recognise scripural testomony as the most important variety of source of knowledge. However in the concluding chapter (XII) scriptural testimony as the source of knowledge has been examined especially with reference to verifiability theory of meaning according to which scriptural sentences lack cognitive significance. In order to encounter such a situation two types of attempts have been considered (S. 12.11) : (A) Traditional approach to scriptural sentences and (B) An approach from the side of use theory of meaning. It has been argued that these approaches are unable to uphold the informative value of scriptural language. However my recent studies in the direction of understanding the nature of scriptural language enable me to sort out the reasons for the cognitive status of scriptural language. Recently authors like Swinburne (1977 : 1-4)[1] have argued for the cognitive status of scriptural language especially with reference to theistic universe of discourse. In the sequeal I shall also consider similar views found in the writings of Quine.

S 2. Swinburne's theory of credal sentences within the theistic framework implies cognitive status of credal sentences which normally constitute the scriptural language of theism. But what is a credal sentence ? And how does it differ from a declarative sentence of ordinary or scientific discourse ? Since credal language is committed to a certain sort of theism;[2] a credal sentence is normally characterised with reference to divine being. Accordingly a credal sentence is a sentence in which God is defined in terms of the list of properties such as (i) there is a divine being without a body; (ii) He (divine person) is present everywhere; (iii) He is a free agent to do everything (omnipotent); (iv) He knows all things (omniscient); (v) He is perfectly good; (vi) He (God) exists. It is said that credal sentences are grammatical sentences so that the words which occur in them are ordinary words used in their usual or normal sense. Even if there are technical terms such as 'omnipotent', credal sentences express their (cognitive) meanings. However Swinburne (1977 : 3-6) thinks that (i) credal language is not intentional as it expresses claims about how things are so that they are also objects for investigation. (ii) Further he also thinks that for a sentence in order to make a factual claim it need not be in some sense vertifiable or fabriable. But, whether (i) and (ii) are coherent ? Normally, whatever is investigated, in some way or the other, is subject to confirmation or confutation. But the author denies the posibility of any corroboration, concerning the factual claims of credal sentences. However, he seems to say something strange but interesting. Firstly he is skeptical about vertifiability principle[3] itself. He does not consider it as a criterion for (factually) meaning of sentences, for many scientific propositions cannot be tested by verifiability principle (Swinburne 1971 : 22). To this effect authors like Popper[4] (1968 : 36-7) think that scientific laws cannot be logically reduced to elementary statements of experience, consequently the criterion of meaningfulness rejects the natural laws as meaningfulness. However search for such natural laws, as Einstein says, is the main task of the physical scientist. And those theories of high level of universality constitute a framework of physical science. Further the concept of meaning in verifiability theory is somewhat dogmatic and arbitrary, for conventionally narrow sense (meaning) is attached to "meaning" used in vertifiability theory so that even any debate about such a concept of meaning will also turn out be meaningless discourse.[5] Swinburne (1977 : 27) gives an interesting imaginary (or possible) counter example to vertifiability principle. According to that example it is possible that a toy kept in a cup-board dances in the mid-night unnoticed by any body. Since there is an absence of a person in the mid-night to confirm or disconfirm the possible state of affair i.e. dancing of a toy; verifiably principle excludes such possibilities. However such an example may not be considered as a genuine counter example to verifiability principle, for even in the absence of any person, it is still possible to record the observations of possible occurrances taking place during that time by means of certain recording machine like automatic camera or an electronic observer. However from a logical point of view if a proposition is the bearer of truth value then truth or falsity of that proposition is independent of empirical considerations. Thus meaning of that proposition is also independent of empirical considerations.

S 3. However Swinburne's (1977 : 27) argument is that credal sentences are factual even if their are no observation statements and evidences of observation could not be counted as for or against credal sentences. Peculiarity of credal sentences is to their structures in terms of their coherent nature. In a body of coherent claims a statement p entials another statement q if and only if p and ~ q are inconsistent. Or p entials q if and only if ~ p and q are also inconsistent. However p entails q and ~ q entails ~ p are consistent with each other. Swinburne's (1977 : 34) concept of coherent statement is narrower than the usual sense that coherent sentence entails true statement only; and inconerent sentences are false; often incoherent sentences are self contradictory. However Swinburne (p 14) appears to be inconsistent when he sayss that analytic and synthetic distinction also holds in case of credal sentences which are coherent statements; those credal sentences whose negations are also coherent are called synthetic credal sentences but those credal sentences whose negations are incoherent are analytic in nature. Now suppose two synthetic statements p and q being coherent entail each other, so that ~ q becomes incoherent and does not fit in the set of credal sentences p and q but the author says ~ q is also coherent and that coherent statement is true, which is odd. Two incoherent statements need not be false to gether one of them me be true.

S 4. However Swinburne (1973 : 30) considers the question whether credal sentences make coherent statements ? An answer to this question presupposes the notion of meaning in order to consider the possibility of meaningfulness of a credal sentence. Accordingly words are meaningful when they are used in standard cases of sentences expressing coherent statements, or meanings of such expressions may be introduced by new syntactic and/or semantic rules. A syntactic rule for an expression 'e' is used in conformity with the general conditions such as verbal definitions. And semantic rule for the usage of an expression 'e' implies coherently given objects to which that 'e' is correctly applied. However these two criteria are more general in nature and hence include other forms of discourse including theistic and non-theistic universes of discourse. Perhaps author's intention is to characterise meaningful expressions of theistic discourse in a conventional way; words are meaningful if they have an established use in laaguage. Further author argues that a sufficient condition of a credal sentence making a statement is that there are ways of arguing for or against what it experesses. However such deliberation may or may not rely on empirical considerations. Further a proof of coherence for a proposition p follows logically or deductively from some other proposition say which is coherent and any possibility of deducing p as contradiction of p from r is ruled out. Swinburne (1977 : 85) thinks that credal sentences seem to imply as if they are making claims about a reality beyond the world of sense. However Swinburne is not clear about the cognitive status of credal sentences.

S 5. Quine (1951 : 1950) has made an interesting case regarding the cognitive status of credal or theistic sentences.[6] He considers the schema '(x) (x exists)' which may turn out to be true or false depending upon a value for variable assigned. He thinks that the resulting statement 'God exists', obtained by assigning 'God' to x in the formula 'x exists'. It may become a controversial conclusion; an atheist may repudiate the very name 'God'. Inorder to avoid the controversy concerning existence or non-existence of God, Quine introduces matrices like [god], and then introduces 'God' as abbreviation of '(x) god x'. Further it is said that if there is a unique object x such that god x i.e. if.

(a) $(\exists y)\ (x)\ (x=y . \equiv \text{godx})$,
then (x) god x is that object.

According to Quine (a) is bearer of the truth values, for instance he says that monotheists and atheists disagree only on the truth values of statements like (a). Quine implies that statements like (a) are cognitively meaningful. Especially for the theists and monotheists the statement (a) is true statement. The statement (a) according to Swinburne also is a true credal sentence.

Thus scriptural language by virtue of coherent credal sentences implies its cognitive nature. Consequently scriptural testimony[8] as a set of true (credal) sentences qualifies itself as a source of knowledge. Autonomy of scriptural testimony is due to knowledge of unique object (SS 8.7-8) it yields which is not derivable from other pramāṇas. Thus scriptural testimony is a genuine pramāṇa.

Notes and References

1. (i) Swinburne R (1977). *The Coherence of Theism,* I edition. Clarendon Press, Oxford. Thc author in this book has made an attempt to argue the issues concerning the cognitive status of religious language with considerable rigor and thoroughness. Most of the ideas of Swinburne are acceptable to (ii) Penelhum T (1980) : 'The Coherence of Theism by R. Swinburne' (Review) in *Journal of Philosophy,* pp. 502-8.

2. A sort of theism, as conceived by Swinburne*:* (*op. cit.*, p. 1), implies belief in God, who is eternally free, knows everything, is perfectly good and is the object of human worship. He is also creater and sustainer of the universe.

3. Swinburne (1977:23) thinks that certain existential statement asserting the existence of a member of an open class need not falsifiable (or verifiable), for instance even if it is possible that 'There is a bird with two heads' one may not collect evidences for and against such a claim. However Swinburne's reasons are not convincing. A certain may be statement existential (and empirical) it is possible consider certain evidences to confirm or disconfirm so that probability of such statement may increase or decrease, accordingly.

4. Popper K.R. (1968) ; *Logic of Scientific Diseovery.* Hutchinson, University Library. London Popper's criticism of verifiability theory of meaning consists in pointing out inapplicability of verifiability principle to non-reducible universal laws of science. Consequently the alleged criterion of meaningfulness rejects genuine scientific laws. And Popper's programme consists in accomoditing non-verifiable scientific statements in the class of scientific statements with reference to adequate characterisation of scientific statements. Popper (p. 313-4) thinks that the dogma of meaning or sense which gives rise to pseudo problem can be eliminated by the criterion of demarcation of scientific proposition. With greater degree of precision the criterion of demarcation distinguishes the theoretical system of emperical sciences from those of metaphysical, conventional and tautological systems without qualifying metaphysical sentences as meaning less. Popper also thinks that from a historical point of view metaphysical systems(s) can be seen to be the source(s) for theories of empirical sciences.

5. (i) Popper, *Op. cit.*, p. 35.

(ii) Quine W.V. (1950) : 'Two dogmas of empiricism' in *Classics in Analytic Philosophy*. Ed. by Ammerman, Tata Mac.Graw Hill, Delhi. pp. 197-212. In this article Quine (197) has argued that the belief that each meaningful statement is reducible to some statements of immediate experience is a kind of dogma for the supposed boundry between speculative metaphysics and natural science is blurring. Quine (212) observes that : "Physical objects are conceptually incorporated into the situation as convenient intermediaries not by definition in terms of experience, but simply as irreducible posits comparable, epistemologically to the Gods of Homer which differ only in degree and not in kind. Both sorts of entities enter our conception only as cultural posits.

6. Authors like Post J.F. (1974) : 'New Foundations for Philosophical theology in *Journal of Philosoohy* (pp. 73-148), have made an attempt to show that Quine's naturalism is liberal to provide an adequate foundation for theology or religious language. That is to say that certain plausible interpretations can be given to the main concepts and theories of philosophy of religion. Post (736-7) hopes that concepts like God, eternity, transcendence, omniscience etc. get their meanings more adequately through Quinean techniques of interpretations. However Quine may not accept all that has been said by Post regarding the interpretation of theological concepts. Quine is very much concerned with logical aspect of theological discourse rather than ontological implications of religious language. This point has been clearly emerged in Quine W.V. (1951) : *Mathematical Logic*, Cambridge Massachusetts, p. 150.

7. In contemporary semantics, especially in one of its branches—theory of reference, an attempt has been made to understand the nature of 'terms like 'God', 'Pegusus' etc. Even though theory of reference is distinguished from theory of meaning (sense), any adequate chararacterisation of theistic and mythological concepts must be from both the sides. Although according to Frege every term having reference necessarily possess sense, it need not be the case that every expression having sense should refer to something. Terms like 'Pegusus' have sense but do not designate any referent. However according to theism the term 'God' designates divine being God and at the same time it possesses sense (as cluster properties) also. However there are alternative theories of reference (by Kripke, Donnellan etc.) where only referential aspect of an expression is considered. One of such theories involving theory of rigid designator may be extended to understand theistic terms like 'God'. The name 'God' rigidly designates divine being God if and only if the terms God refers to God in all possibie worlds.

8. Recently, attempts have been made to understand Śruti (revelation) as a source of (moral knowledge), especially with reference to Karma-Kāṇda (action portion) of Veda. Both Purusottama Bilimoria and J.N. Mohanty claim autonomy to śruti for it is a source of moral imperatives. In his paper Bilimoria p (1985) : Mīmāṃsā on apauruśeya'—A possibility of the trans-personal world IAHR IX Congress, Sydney University, pp. 1-71, has given following reasons for the autonomy of śruti as a source of knowledge (p. 1-2). Revelation points to transpersonal source and scriptural truths (moral) which are irreducible to emprical facts or to descriptive concepts. Śruti as revelation has

also been accepted as source of moral guides and ethical signposts that help in the direction of the development of human integrity and interpersonal justice. To this effect Bilimoria also refers to Prof. J.N. Mohanty's (p. 11-2) that śruti is a product of historical self-reflection involving mass of doctrines of knowledge accumulated over the years. Śruti is not dogmatic but it finds rational defence in the classical schools. Prof. J.N. Mohanty in his presidential aedress on Philosophy and Tradition (delivered on 21st Oct. 86 in Indian Philosophical Congress, held at Jadhavapur University, Calcutta) has stressed the Karma-kāṇda (or imperative aspect) of śruti, (with reference to apauruṣeyata-vāda of Mimāṃsakas). However both the authors stress on Karmakāṇda aspect of śruti without considering Jñāna-kānda part of Veda (śruti). I think it is jñāna-kāṇda of śruti which needs to be understood as a source [of knowledge. And autonomy of sruti is due to unique knowledge it yields. My understanding of śruti is mainly confined to cognitive aspect of śruti. Even though there is a subclass of imperative sentences in śruti, it is a subject matter for further investigation ino rder to understand the structure and function of scriptural imperative in knowledge situations.

BIBLIOGRAPHY

Note : 1. Please see item (c) under B (Conventions), p. iv.

2. The year of publication mentioned in the entries is not necessarily the year of first publication.

1. Acharya, N.R. (1948) : *Brahmasūtra Śāṅkarabhāṣyam.* Third edition. The Nirnaya Sagar Press, Bombay.

2. Alston, W.P. (ed) (1963) : *Religious Belief and Philosophical Thought.* First edition. Harcourt, Brace of World, Inc., New York; Chicago; San Francisco; Atlanta.

3. ——— (1964) : *Philosophy of Language.* First edition. Prentice Hall, Inc., Englewood Cliffs, N.J.

4. ——— (1967) : "Religious Language." *Encyclopaedia of Philosophy,* edited by Edwards. p 7, 168-73. The Macmillan Co. and the Free Press, New York. Collier Macmillan Ltd., London.

5. Anscombe, G.E.M. (1959) : *An Introduction to Wittgenstein's Tractatus,* First Edition. Hutchinson University Library, London.

6. Armstrong, D.M. (1973) : *Belief, Truth and Knowledge.* First edition. Cambridge University Press, London.

7. Armstrong D.M. (1978) : *Theory of Uuiversals and Scientific Realism* (Vol. II). First edition. Cambridge University Press, Cambridge, London, New York, Melbourne.

8. Athalye, Y.V. and M.R. Bodas (eds). (1974) : *Tarkasaṃgraha of Annaṃbhaṭṭa* (with the Author's *Tarkadīpikā and Govardhana's Nyāya-bodhinī*). Enlarged editton. Bombay Sanskrit Series No. 55, Bombay.

9. Ayer, A.J. (1946) : *Language, Truth and Logic*. Fourth edition, (First edition 1936). Dover Publications, Inc., New York.

10. ——— (1977) : *The Problem of Knowledge*. Reprinted. (First edition 1956). Penguin Books Ltd., Harmondsworth, England.

11. Banerjee, N.V. (1974) : *Spirit of Indian Philosophy*. First edition. Arnold Heinemann Publishers, New Delhi.

12. Barlingay, S.S. (1976) : *A Modern Introduction to Indian Logic*. National Publishing House, New Delhi.

13. Bhagāvata, H.R. (ed) (1840) : *Upaniṣadbhāṣyam*. Astekara Co., Pune.

14. Bhatta, G.V. (ed) (1972a) : *Nyāya-siddhānta-muktāvalī*. First edition. M.V. Balaganapati, Mysore.

15. ——— (ed) (1972b) : *Nyāya-siddhānta-muktāvalī*. First edition. M.V. Balaganapati, Mysore.

16. Bhattacharya, C. (1975) : *The Elements of Indian Logic and Epistemology*. Modern Book Agency, Calcutta.

17. Bhattacharya, J.V. (Tr.) (1978) : *Nyāya-mañjarī*. First edition. Motilal Banarsidass, Delhi.

18. Black, M. (1964) : *A Companion to Wittgenstein's Tractatus*. Cambridge University Press, Cambridge.

19. Bloomfield, M. (1972) : *The Religion af the Veda*. Indological Book House, Varanasi.

20. Broad, C.D. (1953) : "The Argument from Religious Experience." *Religious Belief and Philosaphical Thought*, edited by W.P. Alston (1963). 164-72.

21. Brown, R. and Watling, J. (1951) : "Amending the Verification Principle." *Analysis*, 4, 87-9.

22. Burke, T.E. (1978) : Included in Leinfellner, E., W. Leinfellner, H. Berghel and A. Hübner (eds) (1978), 510-2.

23. Chatterjee, S. (1939) : *The Nyāya Theory of Knowledge*. First edition. University of Calcutta.

24. Chisholm, R.M. (1977) : *Theory of Knowledge*. Second edition. Indian Reprint. (First edition 1966). Prentice Hall of India Private Ltd., New Delhi.

25. Church, A. (1956) : *Introduction to Mathematical Logic*. Vol. I, First edition. Princeton University Press, Princeton, N.J.

26. Clark, M. (1963) : "Knowledge and grounds." *Analysis* 24, 46-7.

27. Copi, I.M. (1972) : *Introduction to Logic.* Collier Macmlilan International, New York.

28. Crombie, I.M. (1963) : "Can Theological Statements Be Tested Empirically ?" See Alston (1963), 283-95.

29. Datta, D.M. (1927) : "Testimony as a Method of Knowledge." *Mind.* 36, 354-8.

30. ——— (1963) : "Verbal Testimony as a source of Valid Cognition." *Recent Indian Philosophy.* Bhattacharya, K. (ed) (1963), 201-11. Progressive Publishers, Calcutta.

31. ——— (1972) : *The Six Ways of Knowing.* (First edition 1932). University of Calcutta.

32. Demos, R. (1917) : "A Discussion of a Certain Type of Negative Proposition." *Mind,* 24, 189-95.

33. Deutsch, E. (1969) . *Advaita Vedānta.* First edition. East-West Center Bress, Honolulu.

34. Devaraja, N.K. (1972) : *Śaṅkara's Theory of Knowledge,* Motilal Banarasidass, New Delhi.

35. Feigl, Nerbert, and Wilfrid Sellers (eds) (1949) : *Readings in Philosophical Analysis.* Appleton-Century-Crofts, New York.

36. Flew, A. (1963) : "Can Theological Statements Be Tested Empirically ?" Included in Alston (ed) (1963), 275-7; 281-3.

37. Frege, G. (1977) : "Thoughts". *The Logical Investigations,* First Chapter. Geach, P., and R.H. Stoothoft (ed, trs) (1977). Basil Blackwell, Oxford.

38. Gambhirananda, Swami (tr) (1972) : *Brahma-sūtra-bhāṣya of Śaṅkarācārya.* Second edition. Advaita Āśrama, Calcutta.

39. ——— (tr) (1977) : *Eight Upaniṣads with the Commentary of Śaṅkarācārya* (Vol. I). Fourth impression. Advaita Āśrama, Calcutta.

40. Gettier, E. (1963) : "Is justified true belief knowledge ?" *Analysis,* 23, 121-3.

41. Gurumurti, D. (ed, tr) (1932) : *Saptapadārthī of Śivāditya.* Theosophical Publishing House, Madras.

42. Hamlyn, D.W. (1977) : *The Theory of Knowledge.* (First edition 1970). The Macmillan Press Ltd., London and Basingstoke.

43. Hare, R.M. (1963) : "Can Theological Statements Be Tested Empirically ?" *Religious Belief and Philosophical Thought edited* by Alston (1963), 277-9.

44. Hempel, C.G. (1965) : *Aspects of Scientific Explanation.* Collier Macmillan Ltd., London.

45. ——— (1959) : "The Empiricist Criterion of Meaning." *Logical Positivism.* Ayer, A.J. (ed) (1959). 108-29. The Free Press, New York.

46. Hick, J. (1979) : *Philosophy of Religion.* The Second Indian Reprint. Prentice-Hall of India, New Delhi.

47. Hiriyanna, M. (1952) : *Popular Essays in Indian Philosophy.* Kavyalaya Publishers, Mysore.

48. Hiriyanna, M. (1957) : *Indian Philosophical Studies* (Vol. I and II), Kavyalaya Publishers, Mysore.

49. ——— (1973) : *Outlines of Indian Philosophy.* (First edition 1932). George Allen and Unwin Ltd., Bombay.

50. ——— (1975) : *Indian Conception of Values.* First edition. Kavyalaya Publishers, Mysore.

51. Hospers, J. (1971) : *An Introduction to Philosophical Analysis.* Allied Publisher Ltd., Bombay, Calcutta, New Delhi, Madras, Bangalore.

52. Ingalls, D.H.H. (1951) : *Materials for the Study of Navya-nyāya Logic.* Harvard University Press, Cambridge, Mass.

53. Jha, Ganganatha and Dhundiraja Shastri (eds). (1925) : *The Nyāya-darśhana* (The Sūtras of Gautama and Bhāṣya of Vātsvāyana). Chowkhamba Sanskrit Series Office, Benares.

54. ——— (tr) (1939) : *Gautama's Nyāya-sūtras* (with Vātsyāyana-bhāṣya). Oriental Book Agency, Poona.

55. Jhalkikar, B. (1978) : *Nyāya-kośa.* The Bhandarkar Oriental Research Institute, Poona.

56. Johnson, W.E. (1964) : *Logic* (Vol. II). Dover Publications, New York.

57. Keith A.B. (1977) : *Indian Logic and Atomism.* First Indian edition. (Originally Published by Oxford University Press, 1919). Oriental Books Reprint Cooperation, New Delhi.

58. Leinfellner, E., W. Leinfellner, H. Berghel and A. Hübner (eds) (1978) : *Wittgenstein And His Impact on Contemporary Thought.* First edition. Hölder Pichler Tempsky, Vienna.

59. Madhavananda, Swami (ed, tr) (1972) : *Vedānta-paribhāṣā of Dharmarāja Adhvarīndra.* Fourth edition. Advaita Āsrama, Calcutta.

60. ——— (tr) (1975) : *The Bṛhadāraṇyaka Upaniṣad.* (With *Commentary of Śaṅkarācārya).* Fifth edition- (First edition 1934). Advaita Āśrama, Calcutta.

61. ——— (tr) (1977) : *Bhāṣa-pariccheda* with *Siddhāntamuktāvalī* by Viśvanātha, Nyāya-pañcānana. Third edition. (First edition 1940). Advaita Āsrama, Calcutta.

62. Mahadevan, T.M.P. (1971) : *Outlines of Hinduism.* Chetana Ltd., Bombay.

63. ——— (1976) : *The Philosophy of Advaita.* (Fourth edition 1938). Arnold-Heinemann, New Delhi.

64. Malcolm, N. (1967) : "Wittgenstein, Ludwig Josef Johann." *Enclopaedia of Philosophy*, edited by P. Edwards (1967), Vol. 8, 327-40.

65. Matilal, B.K. (1960) : "The Doctrine of Karaṇa in Grammar and Logic." *Journal of Ganganatha Jha Research* Institute, 17, 63-9.

66. Matilal, B.K. (1968a) : *The Navya-nyāya Doctrine of Negation* First edition. Harvard University Press, Cambridge, Mass.

67. ——— (1968b) : "Indian Theories of Knowledge and Truth." *Philosoyhy : East and West*, 18, 321-6.

68. ——— (1971) : *Epistemology, Logic and Grammar in Indian Philosophical Analysis.* First edttion. Mountain, The Hague Paris.

69. Matilal, B.K. (1977) : "Nyyāa Bhūṣana on Nyāya-sara". Included in Potter, K.H. (ed) (1977), 420-1.

70. Mitchel, B. (1963) : "Are Theological Statements tested empirically ?" Included in *Religious Belief and Philosophical Thought*, edited by Alston (1963), 279-81.

71. Mitchel, B (1978) : *The Justification of Religious Belief.* First edition. Macmillan Press Ltd and Co., London.

72. Mohanty, J.N. (1966) : *Gaṅgeśa's Theory of Truth.* First edition. Visva-Bharati, Santiniketan (West Bengal).

73. Montague, W.P. (1958) : *The Ways of Knowing.* George Allen and Unwin, London.

74. Mullatti, L.C. (1977) : *The Navya Nyāya Theory of Inference.* First edition. Karnatak University, Dharwad.

75. Murty, S. (1974) : *Revelation and Reason in Advaita Vedānta.* (First edition 1959). Motilal Banarsidass, New Delhi.

76. Nielson, K. (1971) : *Contemporary Critique of Religion.* First edition. Prentice Hall, New York.

77. Nikhilananda, Swami (tr) (1974) : *The Māṇḍūkyopaniṣad with Gauḍpāda's Karika and Śaṅkara's Commentary.* Sixth edition. (First edition 1936). Sri Ramakrishna Āśrama, Mysore.

78. Pitcher, G. (1964) : *The Philosophy of Wittigenstein.* Prentice-Hall of India, New Delhi.

79. Pollock, J. (1974) : *Knowledge and Justification.* First edition. Princeton University Press, Princeton, N.J.

80. Popper, K.R. (1968) : *The Logic of Scientific Discovery.* Hutichnson of London.

81. Potter, K.H. (ed) (1977) : *The Encyclopaedia of Indian Philosophy* Vol. II. Motilal Banarsidas, New Delhi.

82. Price, H.H. (1969) : *Belief.* First edition. George Allen and Unwin London.

83. Quinton, A. (1967) : "Knowledge and Belief." *The Encyclopaedia of Philosophy Vol. 4*, edited by p. Edwards (1967), 345-52. The Macmillan Co. and The Free Press, New York. Collier Macmillan Ltd., London.

84. Quine, W.V. (1960) : *World and Object.* The M.I.T. Press, Cambridge, Mass.

85. Quine, W.V. and Ullian J.S. (1970) : *The Web of Belief.* First edition. Random House, New York.

86. Radhakrishnan, S. (1977a). *Indian Philosophy* (Vol. I). Blackie and Sons, Bombay.

87. Radhakrishnan, S. (1977b) : *Indian Philosophy* (Vol. II). Blackie and Sons, Bombay.

88. Raja, K. (1969) : *Indian Theories of Meaning*. Second edition. (First edition 1963). The Adyer Library and Reseasch Centre, Madras.

89. Raja, K.C., and Sastri, S.S. (eds, trs) (1975) : *Mānameyodaya of Nārayaṇa*. Second edition. (First edition 1933). The Adyar Library and Research Centre Madras.

90. Randle, H.N. (1976) : *Indian Logic in the Early Schools*. First edition. (Originally published in 1930 by Oxford University Press). Oriental Books Reprint Corporation, New Delhi.

91. Rorty, R. (1967) : "Intuition." *Encyclopaedia of Philosoyhy*. Edwards, P. (ed) (1967), 4, 204-12. Macmillon Publishing Co., Inc. and The Free Press, New York. Collier Macmillan Publishers, London.

92. Russel, B. (1949) : *Our Knowledge of the External World*. George Allen and Unwin, London.

93. ——— (1971) : "The Philosophy of Logical Atomism." *Logic and Knowledge*. Marsh, R.C. (ed) (1971), 175-281. George Allen and Unwin, London. The Macmillan and Company, New York.

94. Russell, B. (1951a) : *An Inquiry into Meaning and Truth*. Fourth impression. (First edition 1940). George Allen and Unwin, London.

95. ——— (1951b) : *Human Knowledge, Its Scope and Limits*. Second Impression. (First edition 1948). George Allen and Unwin, London.

96. Salmon, W. (1973) : *Logic*. Prentice Hall, New York.

97. Sandal, M.L. (ed, tr) (1923) : *The Mīmāṃsa Sūtras of Jaimini*. First, edition. The Panini Office, Allahabad.

98. Satris, S.A. (1978) : "Wittgenstein and His Impact on Contemporary Thought." Edited by Leinfellner, included in E.W. Leinfellner, H. Berghee and A. Hūbner (eds) (1978), 507-8.

99. Satprakasananda, Swami (1974) : *Method of Knowledge*. First Indian edition. (First edition 1965, George Allen and Unwin Ltd., London). Advaita Āśram, Calcutta.

100. Saunders, J.T. and Champavat, N. (1964) : "Mr. Clark's definition of knowledge." *Analysis*. 25. 8-9.

101. Schlick, M. (1936) : "Meaning and Verification." *Philosophical Review*. 45, 339-68. *Included in* Feigal and Sellers 1949. 146-10. My references are to Feigl and Sellers.

102. Schmidt, P.T. (1961) : *Religious Knowledge*. First edition. The Free Press of Glencoe Ince., New York.

103. Sengupta, S.C. (1978) : *Logic of Religious Lauguege*. First edition. Prajña, Calcutta.

104. Sukla, S, (ed) (1971) : *Nyāya-mañjarī* of Jayanta Bhaṭṭa (Part I). The Choukhamba Sanskrit Series Office, Varanasi.

105. Thalberg, I. (1969) : "In defence of justified true belief." *Journal of Philosophy*, p. 794-303. Vol. 66 No. 22. The Journal of Philosophy Inc., New York.

106. Vidyabhusana, S. (1971) : *History of Indian Logic*. Motilal Banarsidass, New Delhi.

107. Wiggins, D. (1965): "Identity statements" in *Analytical Philosophy*. Second Series. p. 40-71 (edited by R.J. Butler. First edition). Basil Blackwell, Oxford.

108. Wittgenstein, L. (1961) : *Tractatus Logico—Philosophicus*. (First German edition 1921). Pears D.F. and B.F. McGuiness (eds, tr) (1961). Routledge and Kegan Paul, London and New York.

109. ——— (1963) : *Philosophical Investigations*, (translated by G.E.M. Anscombe). Reprint of second edition. (First edition 1953). Basil. Blackwell, Oxford.

110. Woozley, A.D. (1967) : *Theory of Knowledge*. Hutchinson and Co. Ltd., New York.

Sanskrit Index

The following is the combined index of words and names of authors. Figures refer to notes if preceded by page number and 'fn' otherwise they refer to pages.

Dhvani 85
Naiyāyika 4, 18, 19-33, 70, 75, 82, 84, 87, 109
Navya-naiyāyika 25, 26, 27, 28, 66 (fn 5), 65
Navya-nyāya 25-27,
Nigamana 24-5
Nirvikalpaka pratykṣa 23
Nyāya 1, 9, 17, 23, 89
Nyāya bhāṣya 2, 24, 68
Nyāya mañjarī 2, 69
Pakṣa 110
Pakṣa-dharmatā 45, 110
Pada 85
Parataḥ pramāṇya-vāda 66, 107-8, 109, 112-4
Parāmarṣa 27
Pūrva-mīmāṃsā 17, 66, 82, 113
Pratijñā 42
Pratijñā 24, 5
Pratyakṣa 2, 22, 23, 24
Prābhākaras 46, 66-7, 114
Pratiyogī 39, 46, 50, 51
Pramā 2, 3, 8, 16-58
Pramāṇa 8, 59-65, 66, 70, 97
Bhaṭṭas 19, 66, 114
Brāhmaṇa 82-3
Bhuddhi 30 fn., 1, 6
Bhāṣāparcciheda (i) 2,
Mānameyodoya 2
Mimāṃsakas 85
Mīmaṃsa-sutra 2,
Yajur-veda 81-3, 84
Yathārthānubhava 2, 19
Yogaja-pratyasatti 50
Yogyatā 88
Raghunath 51
Rigveda 81-3, 84
Ṛsi 79 fn 6, 84
Laukika-śabda 1&61-2
Varṇa 85-6, 88
Vaidika śabda 10, 50
Vaiśeṣika 25, 60
Viśvanāth 2, 61
Viśeṣaṇatā 48
Vātsyāyana 4, 24, 29, 74, 77, 105
Vaidika Śabda 5, 81-83
Vyāpti 34
Veda 85 18, 84, 88-9, 101, 107
Vedānta-paribhāsā 2, 90
Śabda 74, 85
Śabda-pramā 4, 22, 35-7
Śabda pramāṇa 74-80, 142
Śaṅkar 1, 5, 12, 72, 97, 104
Śāṅkarbhāṣya katopaniṣad 104
Śāñkarabhāṣya brahma-sutra 65 fn 2, 72-3 97
Śānkarabhāsya bṛhadāraṇaka-upaniṣad 72 fn 9, 8 fn 1
Śānkarabhāsya māndukya-upaniṣad 104
Samavāya 47-8
Saṃhitā 82
Saṃyoga 47
Saṃjñā 33, 34
Saṃjñī 33, 34
Saṃnidhi 88
Saṃhita 39
Saṃvādi prvrtti 62
Savikalpaka-jñāna 20, 25
Sāma-veda 81-3, 84
Sāmānya-lakṣaṇa-pratyāsati 32, fn 18, 39
Siddhānta muktāvali 2
Smrati 38, 81-2, 19
Svtah-prāmāṇyvada 60, 65
Śruti 81
Hetu 24-5

English Index

Abextra 108, 123
Absence 45, 49
Absential knowledge 28
Alston W.P. 7, 101, 131-25
Anscombe G.E.M 40
Armastrang D.M. 12-3, 48
Athalye Y. 5, 19, 74, 84, 90
Authoritative person 35, 38
Authority 74,
Ayer A.J. 7, 14, 126
Banerjee. N.V. 108
Basic proposition 127-8
Belief 10-11, 21
Bhattacarya C 48, 74, 87, 105
Bilimoria P 150,
Black M. 40, 147-8
Bloomfeild M. 81
Broad. C.D. 131
Burke I.E. 139-40
Chatterjeee S.C. 108, 115
Chisholm R.M. 12
Church. A 18,, 113, 115, 129
Cognition 5, 20, 25
Consciousness 17
Copi I.M. 24, 79
Counterpositive 46
Credal sentences 143-5
Criterion of independence 70-1
Criteria of truth 107-25
Creterion of unique object 70
Crombi I. M 7, 131-135
Datta D. M 49, 97-8 61, 67-8
Demos R. 40-4
Deustch E 7, 120
Devaraja. N. K 121, 104
Doctrine of extrisic validity of knowledge 60, 70, 80
Fact 39, 40, 44
Flew. A 25
Frege G. 17-8
Gettier E. 2, 11-2
God 76, 88, 87-8-9, 108, 143, 145, 147- 109, 140
Hamlyn D.W. 12, 20, 39
Hare R.M. 14, 5
Hempel C.J. 129-30
Hick J. 5, 7, 19, 90, 101-2, 131
Hiriyanna M. 1, 7, 18, 85, 87, 102, 105, 108
Hosperse J. 97, 103
Ideas platonic world of 8
Identification 33
Identify 49
Ingalls D.H.H. 45, 47, 49
Inference 31 fn., 12
Introspection :8, 60
Intuition 103

Jha G. 69
Johnson W.E. 40, 45
Justification 11-15, 37

Keith A.B. 74,
Knowledge 2, 3, 4, 9, 21-2, 74

Madhavananda S. 7, 8, 15, 20
Matilal B.K. 103, 45-6 48, 111
120
Memory 20, 30, fn. 8
Mahadevan T.M.P. 82, 104
Meaning 87, 127, 129, 133,
137-8-9. 143-4
Mitchal B. 131-34
Mohanty J.N. 120,112, 105 147-7
Montage W.P. 5, 77, 97, 103
Mullatti. L.C. 18, 38
Mundane testimony 81
Murty S. 84, 90-1, 102, 120

Nielson. K. 149

Perception 2, 22-4, 33
Perceptual knowledge 21
Pitcher G. 138
Plato 21, 49
Pollock J. 12, 20, 30 fn. 8
Popper. K.R. 14, 143, 146
Potter. K.H. 25
Price. H.H. 5, 78, 131-2
Principle of verification, 126-30
143
Proposition 22, 126

Quinton A. 15, fn. 3
Quine. W.V. 7, 39, 142, 145, 147
Quine W.V and Ullion J.S. 98
Radhakrisnan. S 83
Raja. K. 86
Reason 101, 103-4
Revelation 101-2-3-4-5, 131
Rorty. R 103
Russell. B 39-44, 50-2
Salmon W 79
Satprakashananda. S 76, 82-3,
102, 111, 121
Schlick. M 126
Scriptural author ty 1
Scriptural testimony 81-3, 88,
87-8, 140, 142-8
Sengupta S.C. 138, 140
Sense 89
Swinburne R. 7, 142-6
Testimony 33, 74-5, 79, 91, 97-8
Thalberg I. 12
Trustworthy person 75
Truth 10, 75, 103, 105, 107, 115
127
Type-token 85, 90
Vicious circle 16, 47
Vidyabhusana. S 74
Wiggins. D. 25
Wittgenstein. L 39-41, 44, 137
139, 140
Woozley. A.D. 39, 54